TRIPLE
Action

UNIT 1 BOOK

SCHOLASTIC INC.

Editor

Jeri Schapiro

Associate Editor

Julia Remine Piggin

Art Director

Carol Steinberg

Design

Martha Clark

Production

Anna Ewing

Curriculum Consultants

Beverly Jones Ashbrook, Director of Reading,

Jefferson County Public Schools

Louisville, Kentucky

Joan Curry, Ed.D., Director of Clinical Training Center,

San Diego State University

San Diego, California

Charles Sherwood, Ed.D., Coordinator of Reading Education

University of Mississippi

University, Mississippi

Illustrations and Photography: Eric Barnes, pp. 49-55, 129-132; Robert Dale, pp. 5-8, 20, 22-23, 34, 46, 58, 82, 102, 113, 124-125, 136, 150, 158; Catherine Huerta, cover, pp. 73-79, 117-121, 141-147; Richard Hutchings, pp. 25-31, 39-43, 93-99, 105-110; Jean-Marie Troillard, pp. 11-17, 61-65.

For reprint permission grateful acknowledgment is made to:
James N. Young, Jr., Trustee of the Estate of James N. Young for the adaptation of "The Wrong House" by James N. Young, copyright 1929 by The Crowell–Collier Publishing Co.
Scholastic Magazines, Inc. for "Today Is the First Day of . . ." by James Shannon, copyright © 1973 by Scholastic Magazines, Inc.

ISBN 0-590-30475-5

TABLE OF CONTENTS

WHAT'S IN STORE?

What is the story about?

Why do the characters do what they do?

What will happen next?

When you read, these kinds of questions pop into your head. You think about the way a character feels or acts. You compare stories to the way things are in real life. And you pick up clues and make guesses about what will happen next.

Sometimes you pick up clues right at the start. Suppose you were about to read ''The Case of the Missing Moped.'' From the title, you'd expect the story to be a mystery. In fact, you'd be pretty surprised if it turned out otherwise.

Story illustrations can also tip you off. Right away, you'd be able to guess if a story took place in the present, past, or future. Picture clues would help you make predictions.

How good are you at tracking down clues from pictures? Here's your chance to find out. Look at the illustrations that follow. Under each one, predict whether the story would be a *romance, mystery, adventure, science fiction*, or *humorous story*. Then list the clues that helped you make your guess.

This story would probably be _____.

Clues: _____.

This story would probably be _____.

Clues: _____.

This story would probably be _____.

Clues: _____.

This story would probably be _____.

Clues: _____.

This story would probably be _____.

Clues: _____.

TITLES CAN TELL

Lotta Stuff is making up the table of contents for a book of short stories. She has decided to divide the book into sections. She begins to write the title of each story under the heading that tells what kind of story it is. All at once, the cat jumps onto the desk, knocking some papers to the floor. Can you help Lotta finish the job?

Here are the titles of some short stories that belong in the book. On the next page is the table of contents Lotta had started. Read each title below. Decide which stories go under which headings. Then write the titles where they belong in the table of contents.

Crazy Eddie Strikes Again! The Story of Harriet Tubman
Blue Faces on Mars The Case of the Stolen Birdcage
Race to the Finish! Hijacked!
The Curse of Hollow Valley Blind Date

TABLE OF CONTENTS

ADVENTURE

Terror at 10,000 Feet

BIOGRAPHY

The Life of Harry Houdini

HUMOR

SCIENCE FICTION

Time Tunnel

LOVE AND ROMANCE

The Velvet Valentine

MYSTERY AND DETECTIVE STORIES

SPORTS

You Win Some, You Lose Some

HORROR

VOCABULARY STUDY

| attendance | cream | fattening | lard | weight |
| couple | diet | gym | sundae | weird |

These words appear in the first story you will read. They also belong in the story below. Write the word that belongs in each space. When you are done, you will have a complete joke.

"You are too fat," the doctor told Pat. "Even your clothes look

_____ and ill-fitting on you. You must go on a

_____ and lose some _____. Keep away

from all _____ foods. Don't eat anything that has

been fried in _____. And don't eat any more ice

_____ _____s."

A few weeks passed. Pat went back to see the doctor.

"Well, I see you are a little thinner," the doctor said.

"Yes," Pat said. "I have kept up perfect _____ at

the exercise _____. I work out a _____

of days a week. Guess what! This morning I touched the floor without

bending my knees."

"That's great," the doctor said. "How did you do it?"

"I fell out of bed!"

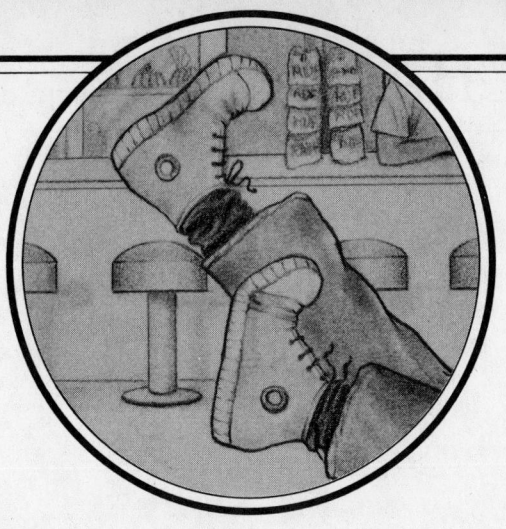

NO
FAT CHANCE

This story is about someone who is always falling — falling in love, that is.

But when Brian "falls" for someone, he does so in a most unusual way....

NO FAT CHANCE by H. William Stine and Megan Stine

There was a new girl in English class. She was tall and very, very thin. Right away we knew she was going to be a little weird.

That first day, the teacher was taking attendance before class. Everyone was just sort of sitting there being quiet.

Suddenly, the new girl stood up and said, "My name is Mercy Danton. I am thin and beautiful. And I never date anyone who weighs more than 130 pounds. No tub of lard is going to block people's view of me. That's my rule, and I never break it."

Then she sat down and class began.

Well, this didn't seem to bother most people. But it bothered Brian

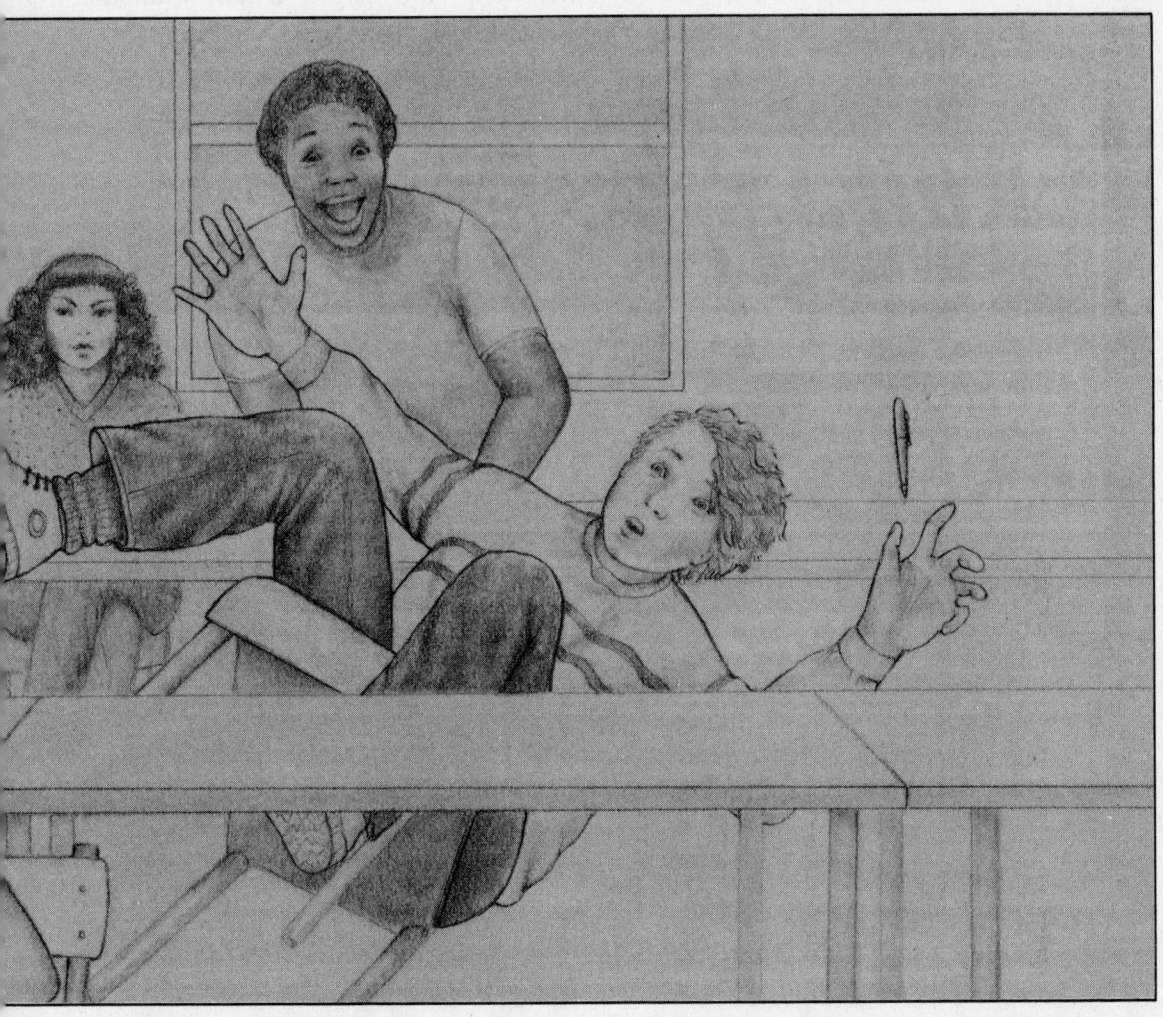

Collins, who fell out of his chair. Everyone knew that meant trouble. Brian Collins only fell out of his chair when he was in love.

The first time it happened was in second grade. Brian fell in love with his teacher, Mrs. Griddle. Every time Brian saw her, he fell out of his chair. It was as simple as that, until one day he fell and broke his arm. Brian swore off women after that. He decided they were too dangerous.

But here he was, falling in love and out of his chair again. Now Brian sure wasn't fat. In fact, he was one of the best-looking guys at school. So he thought he really had a chance with Mercy Danton.

Well, word got around pretty fast about what was going on. People were really worried about Brian. At lunch, everyone brought pillows from the music room. They put them on the floor around Brian so he wouldn't hurt himself when he fell.

Brian didn't talk much. And he didn't eat anything. He fell out of his seat a lot and kept saying, "She's beautiful." He said that over and over. He was in bad shape.

Then Brian and Mercy ran into each other near the gym. Brian walked right over to her (and he only fell twice). "Hi, Mercy," he said.

"Don't stand in front of me," Mercy said.

"Oh, I forgot," Brian said. "You want people to see you."

"Something wrong with that? After all, I am beautiful," Mercy said, smiling.

"How would you like to go out

with me Friday night? What do you say?"

Mercy didn't say anything. She simply led Brian to the scale in the gym office. Brian stepped on the scale. It said 142 pounds.

"Sorry, Tubby, you lose," Mercy told him. Then she walked away.

Brian sat down on one of the chairs in the office. Of course, he fell out of it.

Coach Anderson found Brian on the floor. "What's the matter Brian? Lose something?" Coach Anderson asked.

"No," said Brian. "But you just gave me an idea. How can I lose 12 pounds?"

"You don't need to lose 12 pounds. You're in good shape, Brian."

"Yes, I've got to lose 12 pounds as fast as I can. How can I do it?" Brian asked.

"Well, if you really want to know...start running. Running should do it," Coach Anderson said.

"Great. Thanks, Coach."

The rest of the day and on into the night Brian ran around the track. He missed his dinner. He missed his favorite TV shows. He missed his homework. And worst of all, he missed school the next day.

But when he got on the scale a couple of days later, it said 135 pounds. He had lost seven pounds.

His teachers said, "Why weren't you in class yesterday?"

"I was running," Brian said. "I mean, I was running a fever."

"You know, you don't look very well," they told him. "You look like you lost weight."

"Gee, thanks," Brian said.

Later that day, Brian asked his best friend, Marty, how to lose more weight.

"Brian, you're crazy. You're not fat," Marty said. "But if you really want to lose weight, you should go on a diet."

"A diet? What kind of a diet?" Brian asked.

"Well, the best one is the Rabbit Diet." Marty said. "You eat the things a rabbit eats — lettuce, carrots, and berries."

"But I hate lettuce and carrots. Are you sure this will work?"

"Of course," said Marty. "Have you ever seen a fat rabbit?"

Well, Brian didn't like it, but he decided to try it anyway. For two days he ate nothing but lettuce, carrots, and berries. He ate so much of the stuff, he was afraid he'd grow long white ears and a tail.

But on Friday morning, the scale said 130 pounds. He'd made it! He knew Mercy Danton would finally go out with him.

At school Brian waited for Mercy in the gym. When she came in, he went

to the scale in the office. Everyone followed them.

"129½ pounds," Brian said with a smile. "Now will you go out with me, Mercy?"

Everyone waited for the answer.

"Are you kidding? Never in a million years," Mercy said.

"But look how thin he is," everyone said.

"That's what I mean," Mercy Danton said. "If I went out with you, do you know what would happen?"

"Yeah, we'd have a good time," Brian said.

"A good time? Everyone would talk about how thin you look and how much weight you lost," Mercy said. "They wouldn't say a thing about me. They wouldn't even notice me! And when I go out, I want people to notice me."

Brian couldn't believe his ears after everything he had done for her. He just stood there for a minute.

Finally Brian said, "Mercy, go soak your head in a hot fudge sundae."

The thought of something fattening must have been too much for Mercy

Danton. She screamed and ran out of the office.

Everyone started laughing then — even Brian. We knew it was over. No more diets, no more falling out of his chair.

"You know," he said. "A hot fudge sundae sounds pretty good."

So we carried Brian on our shoulders to the ice cream shop. And we took turns feeding him hot fudge sundaes. When he finished the first, we bought him another. And Brian said his fourth was as good as the first.

"And I'm swearing off women, you guys. They're too dangerous," said Brian, starting an ice cream cone.

But just then a new girl walked into the shop.

"I'm swearing off women," he said again. "I'm swearing off women." And he said it over a hundred times.

But when the new girl smiled at him, Brian fell out of his chair.

READING CHECK

Directions: When answers are given, put the letter for the right answer in the space. When answers are *not* given, write your answer in the space.

WORD MEANING FROM CONTEXT

1. Brian and Mercy "ran into each other near the gym." This means that ____ .
   a. they crashed into each other
   b. they knocked each other down in the gym
   c. they happened to meet by the gym

2. The sentence "He was in bad shape" means that ____ .
   a. Brian had a bad weight problem
   b. Brian was all mixed up
   c. Brian got hurt in an accident

MAIN IDEA

3. This story is about someone who _____

   _____ .

DETAILS

4. Mercy told Brian that he had to lose _____ pounds.

5. Brian lost weight by _____ and _____ .

SEQUENCE

6. Brian had four hot fudge sundaes after Mercy _____

_____ .

FINDING PROOF

7. Mercy was very self-centered. Proof is that _____

_____ .

CAUSE AND EFFECT

8. If Brian fell off his chair, it meant that he _____ .

WHAT DO YOU THINK?

What kind of story is this? Are you supposed to take it seriously? How do you think the author wants you to feel?

Why did Brian say that he was "swearing off women"? Do you think he meant what he said? What happened at the end of the story?

WORDS WITH MORE THAN ONE MEANING

What makes this conversation funny? For one thing, the word *crack* can have more than one meaning. It can mean:

1. to collapse or break from strain

2. a nasty remark

The conversation is funny because it brings both meanings to mind. Many words you read have more than one meaning. How do you decide which meaning is intended? You can usually tell by seeing how the word is used in a sentence.

Each of the following examples gives more than one meaning for a word. Then there are sentences that use the word. Decide which meaning is being used in each sentence. Write the number of the meaning before the sentence.

fast: 1. Rapid; swift. 2. Fixed; non-fading. 3. To eat little or no food.

_____ He practically *fasted* on the diet.

_____ Are the colors in this shirt *fast*?

_____ If you're *fast*, you may get there on time.

late: 1. Not on time; after the usual or expected time. 2. Toward the end of a period of time. 3. No longer living.

____ We will get together *late* in the summer.

____ The *late* Pat Smith used to like bowling.

____ The class started *late* today.

dash: 1. To run or rush suddenly. 2. A short race. 3. A little bit. 4. To ruin or destroy.

____ I won the 50-yard *dash* in school.

____ Use just a *dash* of pepper in the stew.

____ Brian's hopes of dating Mercy were *dashed*.

____ She *dashed* out of the room, screaming.

medium: 1. In a middle place; neither top nor bottom; neither large nor small. 2. A means through which something is done. 3. A person thought to be a messenger between spirits of the dead and living people.

____ TV is a powerful *medium* of communication.

____ The *medium* said she had a message from George Washington.

____ *Medium*-priced clothes are on the second floor.

log: 1. A length of wood cut from a tree. 2. To cut trees into lengths of wood. 3. A book in which the daily progress of a ship is written. 4. To enter facts in a ship's record book.

____ The *log* showed how long the ocean voyage took.

____ We need another *log* for the fire.

____ The Captain *logged* how far the ship went today.

____ We would *log* trees for six hours a day.

The following riddles may not *crack you up*. But *take a crack* at them anyway. In each riddle, circle the word that makes the riddle funny. Then write the two meanings for that word.

1. What kind of robbery is the least risky?
   A safe robbery

   _____   _____

2. How do you know if a train has just passed?
   You can see its tracks.

   _____   _____

3. What is strange about the way a horse eats?
   It eats best when it doesn't have a bit in its mouth.

   _____   _____

4. What's the difference between a child and a duck?
   A child grows up and a duck grows down.

   _____   _____

5. Why would a thief in jail want to catch the measles?
   So he could break out.

   _____   _____

6. Why is tennis such a noisy game?
Because someone is always raising a racket.

_____   _____

7. Why is a coward like a leaky faucet?
They both run.

_____   _____

8. What did the picture say when it was hung?
"I was framed!"

_____   _____

9. Why do ghouls make such good writers?
They are always digging up plots.

_____   _____

The words below appeared in the story "No Fat Chance." Reread the story to see how each word was used. Then choose five words. Make up sentences that use the words in different ways. If you get stuck, look up the words in a dictionary.

chance	couple	fast	pound	run	shape	track
coach	fall	notice	pretty	scale	sound	weight

VOCABULARY STUDY

boyfriend   engaged   luggage   program   TV
cancelled   enlisted   managed   there's   unpack
corporal   handsome   problem   tightrope wallet

Write the word that matches each meaning below. Then see if you can find all the words in the word puzzle. The words go ↓ →

something to
carry money in _____

good looking _____

called off _____

a show _____

there is _____

planning to be
married _____

soldier with two stripes
on sleeve _____

signed up in _____

home screen _____

bags for
taking trips _____

steady date _____

take out of a bag _____

something that is difficult
to deal with _____

line stretched in a
circus tent _____

handled or
carried out _____

```
E  C  O  R  P  O  R  A  L  M  H  T  B
N  A  U  W  R  T  T  W  U  A  A  I  X
G  N  N  R  O  V  H  A  G  N  N  G  P
A  C  P  Q  G  S  E  L  G  A  D  H  R
G  E  A  L  R  O  R  L  A  G  S  T  O
E  L  C  Y  A  U  E  E  G  E  O  R  B
D  L  K  T  M  R  S  T  E  D  M  O  L
O  E  N  L  I  S  T  E  D  L  E  P  E
U  D  B  O  Y  F  R  I  E  N  D  E  M
```

PICTURE OF A SOLDIER

Suppose you felt lonely and left out. Suppose you could change all that by telling a little white lie.

That's what Jenny did, and it worked. The trouble was, she found out that lies are like potato chips. You can't stop at just one.

PICTURE OF A SOLDIER

by Julia Remine Piggin

"Is Tom going to be able to get a leave this Christmas?" Karen asked.

Jenny swallowed hard. She made herself look sad. "No," she said. "It's just awful. He's over there in Germany, and he just can't get home. I'm beginning to hate the Army. I haven't seen him in nearly six months."

"Well, cheer up, he still loves you," said Bill, Karen's boyfriend. You've got enough letters to fill a trunk."

"But I can't go out with letters," Jenny said.

Later, in her room, she took out her wallet. She looked at the picture of the young soldier that she always carried. He wasn't exactly handsome. But he looked lively, and different. Now, the dark eyes seemed to laugh at her. "Don't you wish you knew who I was?" they said.

Jenny did not know the soldier in the picture. She had found the picture in a big cardboard box. The box had been left by the movers for her family to pack in. They had moved to Madison in September.

In her home town, Jenny had dated and had fun. But in Madison High, everyone seemed to be paired off. She made some good girlfriends. But by November, she still had not had a date.

One day Karen and Mary were talking about their guys. Jenny opened her purse, and took out her wallet. "Did I ever show you my Tom?" she asked.

She had put the picture in her wallet just for fun. But now, showing it made her feel a lot better. Karen and Mary thought "Tom" was good-looking. "I'll tell you a secret, if you'll promise not to tell anyone," Jenny said. "When he gets out of the Army, we're going to get engaged."

Everything seemed different after that. Jenny still had no dates. But now, it wasn't because boys didn't like her. It was because she was being true to Tom. She began to make up more and more stories about him. She talked about the good times they had had before he enlisted. When her grandmother sent her a sweater, she said Tom had sent it from Germany. "He always said green was my color," she told the girls.

Once, she even told them that Tom was coming home on leave. Then, she almost cried when the leave was "cancelled" at the last minute.

Karen's father worked at the same plant as Jenny's father. One night, Jenny's dad came home and took her aside. "Honey," he said, "Art Norman says his daughter told him that you're engaged to a soldier. What's this all about?"

Jenny hated to lie to her dad. But she had to. "Oh, Dad," she said, "Karen's always getting things mixed up. There's a girl named Jenny Toolan in school. She goes with a soldier in Germany. That's who Karen must have meant. You know I don't go out with soldiers."

The next day, she got Karen alone. "Karen," she said, "there's a problem about Tom. My parents don't like him. I have to get up early and get the mail so they won't see his letters. When he gets back, we'll get it all straight. But now I just don't tell them anything about him."

"I'm sorry, Jen," Karen said. "Me and my big mouth. I'll tell my dad I made a mistake."

After that, Jenny began to feel like she was walking on a tightrope. Any minute, the truth might come out. What would the girls say if they knew? It was too awful to think about. She tried not to talk much about Tom. But when other girls talked about boys, she felt so left out. So she made up more stories. She watched every program about the Army on TV. She was afraid she would say something wrong. Tom was beginning to seem real to her. And sometimes she hated him.

It happened the week before Christmas. Jenny was in the living room reading. She stopped when she heard Bill's little car pull up. Karen jumped out one side. Bill and another boy jumped out the other. Jenny didn't know the other boy. He was tall and handsome. Jenny went to the door, and opened it as they ran up.

"Oh, Jen," Karen cried. "Guess what? The most wonderful surprise! Maybe I shouldn't tell you, but I just have to. He's here! He's here at the airport! He looks just like his picture." The three came into the room.

Jenny felt her legs go weak. "Who?" she said faintly.

"Your man!" Bill said. "The guy in the picture — Tom. We went out to the airport to meet my brother, Lew, here. He's home from college for the holidays. That's where we saw Tom."

"It couldn't be anybody else." Karen's smile was warm. "It was your Tom, all right. Did you know he's been made a corporal? We saw the stripes. That's a surprise, too, I'll bet. We would have offered him a ride. But Lew had luggage and he did too. There wasn't room in the car. Say, I'll bet there's a great present in one of his bags for you!"

It was the end of the world. Jenny looked at them dumbly. She could not speak. What could she say? She sat down on a chair. She tried to talk — and instead, began to cry.

"Oh, she's crying because she's so happy," Karen said to Bill.

"No." Jenny shook her head. "No —it's—" She could not go on. She sobbed.

Karen's face changed. Bill took Karen's hand.

"Karen," he said, "she's trying to tell you something. Jen," he said, bending over Jenny, "did you break up with Tom? Is that what it is!"

Jenny felt like a drowning person being helped into a boat.

"Yes," she managed to say. "Yes, he wrote last month and — I — I just couldn't tell anybody. I hoped — I was so — " She began to cry again.

"Oh, Jenny," Karen said, "how awful. You poor kid. And right at Christmas too. You knew he was coming, and wouldn't see you and — oh, Jenny. You should have told us. We understand. It — it happens.''

Lew came over and lifted Jenny's chin. He looked at her wet face.

"That guy's crazy," he said. "If he threw over a pretty kid like you, he's just plain nuts. Look, I have to get home now, see the folks, and unpack. But how about my borrowing the car and coming over tonight? You and I can go somewhere. If you feel up to it, we can take in a movie. I don't know what there is to do in town, but we'll find something. Or if you just want to tell me all about it, I'll listen.''

Jenny looked up at Lew in shock. For a second, she did not understand what was happening. Then, she felt a wild, crazy joy.

She was being asked for a date. Her first date since she moved to Madison.

And she did not even dare to smile.

READING CHECK

WORD MEANING FROM CONTEXT

1. Jenny's father worked in a *plant*. This means that _____ .
   a. he was a gardener
   b. he worked underground
   c. he worked in a factory

MAIN IDEA

2. This story is about _____ .
   a. someone who is in love with a soldier and loses him
   b. someone who dreams of a soldier who doesn't really exist
   c. someone who learns that telling lies is dangerous, but is saved by a stroke of luck

DETAILS

3. Jenny got Tom's picture when _____ .

4. Jenny's _____ worked at the same place as

   _____ .

SEQUENCE

5. Karen, Bill, and Lew came to Jenny's house after _____

   _____ .

FINDING PROOF

6. Jenny was ashamed of not having dates. Proof is that _____

_____.

CAUSE AND EFFECT

7. Jenny was upset that her friends saw Tom at the airport. The reason

is that _____.

WHAT DO YOU THINK?

Did Lew ask Jenny out because he liked her? Or was he just feeling sorry for her? What makes you think so? If Jenny and Lew go on dating, do you think she should tell him the truth about ''Tom''? Why or why not?

Was making up stories about the picture a bad thing to do? Was it a good thing? Or was it something that didn't matter much one way or the other?

WORDS IN CONTEXT

Sometimes a word, or a group of words, can have different meanings. The meaning depends on how the word or words are used in context. For example, suppose you heard the following. What would you think?

"Tomorrow I will shoot you."

Now suppose you found out that a photographer was talking to a model. Does the message take on a different meaning?

Read the sentences that follow. Underline the words that have the same meaning as the boldface words in the sentences.

1. "If you don't study, you'll be **skating on thin ice**."

walking on broken glass   taking chances   on the wrong pond

2. "I wish you would **drop me a line** every week or so."

throw me a rope   write me a letter   give me a fishing line

3. "As I watched the movie **my heart was in my mouth**."

I was afraid   I felt sick   I was eating candy hearts

4. "When I won the prize, I was **dancing on air**."

very happy   falling out of a window   walking on a soft rug

5. "We sat around all afternoon and **chewed the fat**."

had a big meal   talked a lot   ate pork rinds

6. "Keep quiet and don't **stick your neck out**."

wear a warm hat   risk trouble   hit your head

7. "I can't see you this afternoon. **I'm all tied up**."

very busy   wrapped in rope   stuck to a seat

8. "Thank you for **footing the bill**."

stepping on money   paying for something   jumping up and down

9. "The new kid must be **handled with kid gloves**."

patted on the back   wearing children's clothes   treated very gently

10. "**Keep your chin up**. Your luck will change."

be brave   wear a neck brace   look up at the sky

The following sentences are from "Picture of a Soldier." Check what you think each one means.

Jenny began to feel like she was walking on a tightrope.

_____ a. She felt dizzy all the time.

_____ b. She was afraid she might say something that would give her away.

_____ c. She had decided to train for a job in the circus.

It was the end of the world.

_____ a. Mountains fell.

_____ b. Something bad happened.

_____ c. Someone died.

Jenny felt like a drowning person being helped into a boat.

_____ a. She was all wet.

_____ b. She was out of breath.

_____ c. She was suddenly safe.

Here are some more sentences from the story. Write what you think each sentence means.

"If he threw over a pretty kid like you, he's just plain nuts."

_____

She goes with a soldier in Germany.

_____

Karen's face changed.

_____

VOCABULARY STUDY

ambition   assistant   promotion
apologize   chef   realize

Write the words in the puzzle below. When you are done, you will have a word that is a clue to understanding the next story.

a. one who helps   _ _ _ _ _ □ _ _ _

b. a skilled cook   _ _ □ _

c. desire to do well   _ □ _ _ _ _ _ _

d. express regret for   _ □ _ _ _ _ _ _ _
   a mistake

e. to understand clearly   _ □ _ _ _ _ _

f. an advance or raise   _ □ _ _ _ _ _ _ _
   in position

The title of the story is "Keeping Cool."
What do you think the story will be about?

_____

_____

_____

MAKING PREDICTIONS

Here's how the story begins. Does the opening back up your prediction so far? If not, take another guess.

> **They passed over Slug Curtis and gave me the job. Boy was he mad! Slug was in line for it. He had worked at Don's Burger Palace longer than I had.**
> **I didn't really expect the job, but I wasn't about to turn it down. When Don tells you to do something, you do it.**

Can you guess what will happen next? Can you make some predictions about what you will find out in the story?

The following sentences are predictions made from the information given in the paragraphs above. Some predictions are probable. They seem to go along with the information given. Others are not probable—if there is nothing in the paragraphs to support them.

Try testing yourself. Put a check in front of the predictions that make sense.

_____ 1. Don's Burger Palace will go out of business.

_____ 2. As time goes on, Slug will become very jealous.

_____ 3. You will find out how the person telling the story handles the new job.

_____ 4. The person telling the story will have a problem getting along with Slug.

_____ 5. Slug will quit his job.

_____ 6. Slug will get sick after eating a burger.

Now read the story and check out your hunches.

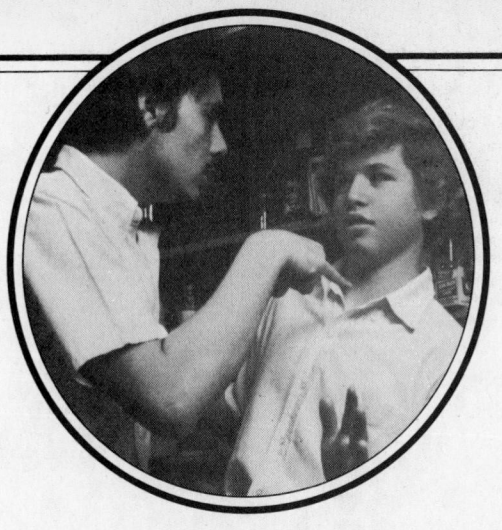

KEEPING COOL

What do you do if you want to get ahead on the job — and somebody starts making trouble? Pete had to come up with an answer. But was it the right one?

KEEPING COOL
by Herma Werner

They passed over Slug Curtis and gave me the job. Boy, was he mad! Slug was in line for it. He had worked at Don's Burger Palace longer than I had.

I didn't really expect the job, but I wasn't about to turn it down. When Don tells you to do something, you do it.

Don is the owner of the place. He's big and rough-talking. Everybody knows how great his burgers are. So people are always in there, buying them by the ton.

I might have been a good guy and refused the promotion. It wasn't the first job I ever had, and it wouldn't be the last. I might have said I didn't want the raise that went with it. But I'm not crazy. I may be a little wild now and then. But I'm not crazy. Anyway, there was something about Slug that I never liked.

So I became assistant part-time chef. That meant staying in the kitchen and helping with a lot of cleaning, cutting, and cooking. I enjoy that sort of thing. There is a future in it. And I've got big plans for my future. There are places where you can learn fancy cooking. All a guy needs is ambition.

You can tell by Slug's name that he's slow. He isn't crazy about work either. So I went into the kitchen while Slug stayed out front and took orders.

There are no tips to speak of in a fast food place. So it didn't take Slug long to get really mad. He didn't get mad at Don or the manager. He got mad at me!

I was in the kitchen peeling onions. We've got this machine that cuts onions. But at Don's, I'm the machine that peels them first. Speed counts for everything. Flip! Flop! Done! That's the way I do things. Once you get going, things really move.

When Don told me I had the job, I took a quick look over at Slug. He heard all right. He stopped what he was doing and stayed very still. His back was to us. I didn't have to see his face to know how he felt. I would have felt the same way.

"Keep up the good work, Pete," Slug said, sneaking up on me. "You'll get to own the place one day."

"I got that in mind," I said, giving him a grin. I was trying to stay cool. What was I supposed to do? Apologize to Slug because I got a promotion? What did they make me, anyway? President of the United States? I stayed cool, I'm telling you, real cool.

Slug didn't say anything. In fact, he didn't talk to me for a week. Suddenly, I was like a piece of plate glass to him. He didn't really see me, and he would walk around me if we came close.

After a week, he was still bugged. I was in the kitchen cleaning up when I felt something at my back. It was Slug.

"Hey, Pete, there's a little spot you missed," he said, pointing to the sink.

"Sure thing, Boss," I said. I took the sponge and wiped the spot away. "Good thing you told me about that," I said. "Got to watch those germs."

"I'm watching a germ right now," Slug said. He was staring at me hard.

I smiled. Nothing was going to bug me, I told myself.

The place was almost empty. And the chef had already gone home. That's the difference between being the big guy and the assistant. The assistant gets to clean up the mess.

The manager and the other guys were out front somewhere. In fact, nobody was in the kitchen but Slug and me. It seemed as if Slug had paid everybody to stay out of there.

"You don't take a guy's job away," Slug said. "You know that?"

"What are you talking about?" I asked. "I'm here minding my own business. I didn't ask for that job. They *gave* it to me."

"You don't work for a month, then move right into the first slot that opens up," he said. "You wait your turn, like everybody else."

Slug was slow I told you that. But he was also big. He had these eyes like a snake. They made him look half asleep, but also mean. He talked slow too. You had to wait a long time until he got everything out. It took me a little while to realize he meant business.

All of a sudden, he slid his hand into his pocket. What would you have done if you thought what I did? Just what I did!

I grabbed the peeler off the counter. I'm fast, remember?

Slug screamed. In a flash, Don and the manager were all over me. They had me around the neck with my arms pinned back.

Slug said he had just been reaching for his handkerchief. It seemed like a set-up to me. I felt like peeling him, just like that onion.

So I lost the job at Don's Burger Palace. Well, it wasn't the first one.

I've got this new job now. It looks real good. Man, I work, I really work. The boss tells me to "keep up the good work." He says I may get to be manager of Fast Frank's some day.

The only trouble is this guy Bo. He's an order clerk like me and he really bugs me. Some guys are like that, you know. Just thinking about them drives you up the wall. But this time I'm going to keep cool. No matter what happens, I'm going to keep cool.

READING CHECK

WORD MEANING FROM CONTEXT

1. In this story, the word *cool* means _____ .
   a. lacking in warmth
   b. calm and self-controlled
   c. excited

2. "I was like a piece of plate glass to him" means _____ .
   a. he thought he could smash me
   b. he seemed to look right through me
   c. I was dangerous

MAIN IDEA

3. This story is about someone who _____

   _____ .

DETAILS

4. The duties of an assistant part-time chef are _____

   _____ .

SEQUENCE

5. Pete went to work at Fast Frank's after _____

   _____ .

FINDING PROOF

6. Pete has a bad temper. Proof of this is _____
   _____ .

CAUSE AND EFFECT

7. Pete smiled when Slug called him a germ because ____ .
   a. he thought it was funny
   b. he didn't want to get into a fight
   c. he wanted to make Slug mad

WHAT DO YOU THINK?

Slug said he had been reaching for his handkerchief. Do you believe him? Why or why not? Pete says that all a guy needs is ambition. Do you think Pete needs more than just ambition? What? Pete said this wasn't his first job. Why do you think he may have left his other jobs? What problems might Pete have on his new job? How do you think he will handle them?

CAUSE AND EFFECT

The first picture shows that something has happened. Why did it happen? Look at the next three pictures. Which one caused Dr. Jekyll to turn into Mr. Hyde?

If you picked the third picture, you are right. Here is why:

Dr. Jekyll turned into Mr. Hyde **because** of what he drank.

The drink was the **cause** or reason that something happened.

The **effect** is the thing that happened — that Dr. Jekyll turned into Mr. Hyde.

In reading, it is important to be able to see both the cause and the effect. To find the cause, ask yourself: *What happened? Why did it happen?* To find the effect, ask yourself: *What was the result?*

The eight sentences below are ideas about Pete's work. Four sentences are possible causes for his working. The others are possible effects of his work. They are not in any order. You can separate the causes from the effects by asking yourself: *Is this sentence a possible reason why Pete worked? Or is it a possible result of his work?*

Try testing yourself. If the sentence tells why Pete might have worked, write **cause** in the space before it. If the sentence tells a possible result of his work, write **effect** in the space.

_____ 1. Pete wanted to know what working was like.

_____ 2. Pete bought himself a car.

_____ 3. Pete saved $100.

_____ 4. His father was in the hospital.

_____ 5. Pete met a lot of people at work.

_____ 6. Pete got out of school early.

_____ 7. Pete shared his pay with his family.

_____ 8. Pete wanted money for college.

In reading, you should be able to see why something happened and what resulted from it. In "Keeping Cool," Pete was promoted over Slug. Why? Can you think of some reasons? Write them below.

_____

_____

What happened as a result of his new job? Can you think of some effects? Write them below.

_____

_____

VOCABULARY STUDY

A woman has been found guilty of a crime. She even admits it. But the judge must free her anyway. Why?

To find the answer, read each sentence below. As you read each new word, decide how many **syllables** you hear. Then circle the letter in the correct column. The circled letters will spell out the answer to the brainteaser. The first one is done for you.

	Syllables		
	One	**Two**	**Three**
1. My **suitcase** is all packed.	T	Ⓢ	E
2. **Ain't** means *am not*.	H	P	U
3. A **detective** looks for clues.	W	R	E
4. The **joint** in my finger is stiff.	I	A	B
5. Come down to police **headquarters**.	R	F	S
6. I received an **official** letter.	L	Y	A
7. Meet me at the phone **booth**.	S	N	Z
8. Do you **doubt** my word?	I	E	H
9. She is a used car **dealer**.	E	A	C
10. The plan is too **risky**.	V	M	O
11. When I saw the bill, I was **amazed**.	H	E	B
12. Now I work in the sales **division**.	I	W	S
13. I get **nervous** when I'm late.	T	E	D
14. The **salesroom** was crowded.	E	T	A
15. The old **gent** walked slowly.	W	R	P
16. He was a **sergeant** in the army.	T	I	Q
17. I have my driving **license**.	G	N	K

THE WRONG HOUSE

Hasty Hogan and Blackie Burns were on a lucky streak. They had stolen a lot of money and found a safe place to hide it. But they had no idea how safe a place it really was.

THE WRONG HOUSE by James N. Young

The night was dark. And the house was dark. The two men raced toward it. They reached the porch and leaped up the steps. In the shadows they waited, listening.

Silence. Then a whisper: "We can't stay out here. Grab this suitcase. Let me try them keys. We got to get in!"

Ten — twenty — thirty seconds. The door opened. The two men went in. Quickly, they closed and locked the door. They wondered if they had awakened anyone in the house.

Finally, one of them said, "Oh, there ain't nobody awake. Let's have a look at this joint." He shined a flashlight around the room. Rugs were rolled up on one side. The furniture

was covered with sheets. Dust was everywhere.

The man with the flashlight spoke first. "Well, Blackie, we're in luck. Looks like the family is away."

"Yep. Gone for the summer, I guess. We'd better make sure, though, Hasty."

Together they searched the house.

There could be no doubt about it. The family *was* away and had been away for weeks.

Yes, Hasty Hogan and Blackie Burns were in luck. Only once in the past ten days had their luck failed them. Luck had been with them when they had made their big haul on the Coast. It had been with them during their long drive east. It had been with them every moment — but one.

That moment had come just an hour ago. It came when Blackie Burns, driving the car, ran over a cop. And Blackie, thinking of the suitcase at Hasty's feet, had raced away.

There had been a chase, of course. When a bullet had put a hole in the tank, they'd had to get rid of the car. And here they were, without a car in a strange town. But they were alive — with a suitcase that held nearly three hundred thousand dollars.

"Listen," said Hogan, "we've got to get a car, fast. It's too risky to steal one. We've got to buy one. That means we've got to wait until the dealers open in the morning."

"What are we going to do with that?" Burns pointed to the suitcase.

"Hide it right here. It's a lot safer here than with us — until we get that car."

And so they hid the suitcase down

in the cellar. They buried it deep in the coal bin.

The next morning, just before dawn, they left.

"Say, Blackie," Hogan said as they walked down the street. "The name of the gent we're visiting is Samuel W. Rogers."

"How do you know?" Burns asked.

"I saw it on some of them books in the living room," Hogan told him.

The car salesrooms opened at eight. Before nine, Hogan and Burns had a car. The dealer lent them his license plates, and they rode away.

Three blocks from the house, they stopped. Hogan got out and walked toward the house. Fifty yards from the house, he stopped. The front door was open. The shades were up. The family had come back!

What a rotten break! What could they do? Break into the cellar that night and grab the suitcase? No, too risky. Hogan would have to think of something.

"Leave it to me," he told Burns. "You drive, and I'll do the brain-work."

Ten minutes later, Hogan was in a phone booth, looking in a phone book. Yes, there it was — Samuel W. Rogers, Plainview 6329. A moment later, he was talking to the surprised Mr. Rogers.

"Hello," he began. "Is this Samuel Rogers?"

"Yes, this is Mr. Rogers."

Hogan cleared his throat. "Mr. Rogers," he said, "this is Police Headquarters. I am Sergeant Simpson of the Detective Division — "

"Yes, yes!" came over the wire.

"The Chief of Police has ordered me to visit your house," Hogan said.

"Am I in any trouble?" asked Mr. Rogers.

"No, no. But I must talk to you."

"Very well," said Mr. Rogers.

"And, Mr. Rogers," Hogan warned. "Please keep quiet about this.

Don't say anything to anybody. You'll understand why when I see you."

On the way, Hogan explained his idea to Burns. Ten minutes later, "Sergeant Simpson" and "Detective Johnson" were talking to the amazed Mr. Rogers. Mr. Rogers was a small man. He had pale blue eyes. He was very nervous — a badly frightened, little man.

Hogan told the story, changing the facts quite a bit. Mr. Rogers was shocked. He led Hogan to the cellar. Together they dug up the suitcase and took it to the living room. They opened it and found that it really did hold a small fortune.

Hogan quickly closed the suitcase.

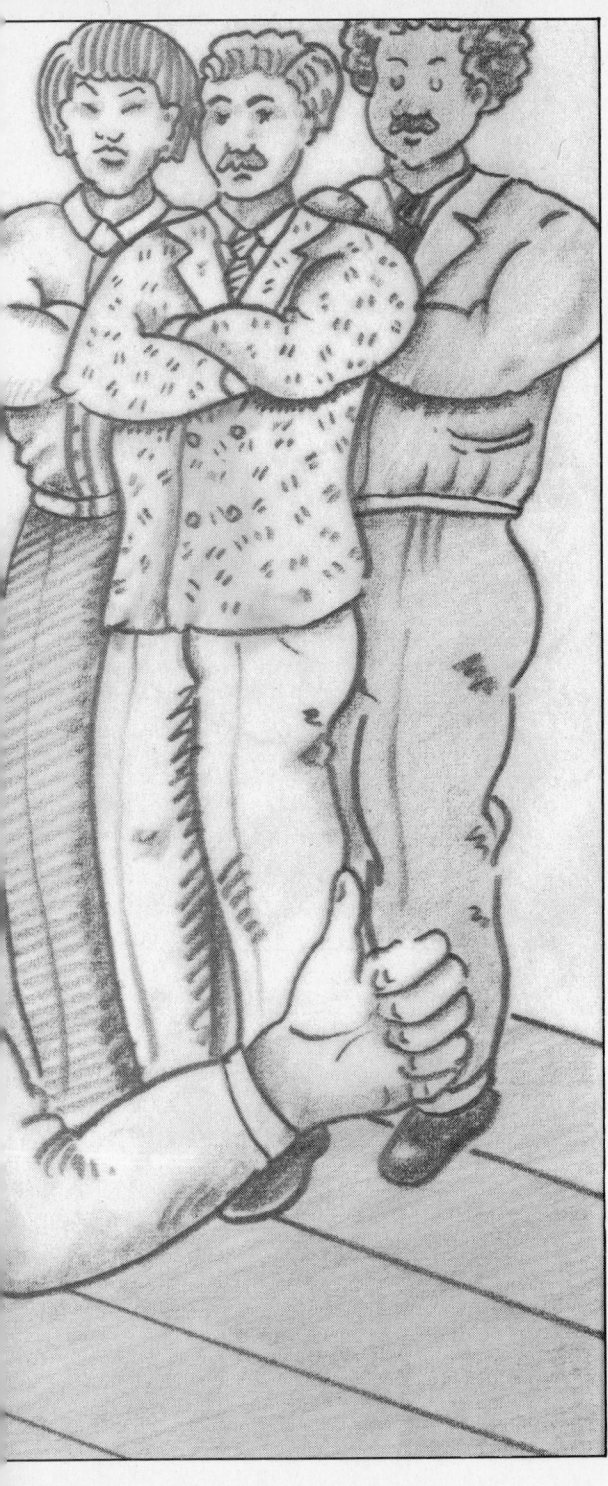

"And now, Mr. Rogers," he said in his best *official* voice, "Johnson and I must run along. We've got to catch the rest of the gang. I'll keep in touch with you."

He picked up the suitcase and walked to the door. Burns and Mr. Rogers followed. Then Mr. Rogers opened the door.

"Come in, boys," he said. In walked three large, strong men. The men stared hard at Hasty Hogan and Blackie Burns.

"What does this mean, Mr. Rogers?" gasped Hogan.

"It's very simple," said Mr. Rogers. "*I* am the Chief of Police."

READING CHECK

WORD MEANING FROM CONTEXT

1. "Let's take a look at this joint." In the story, the word *joint* means ____.
   a. the part between two bones
   b. a cigarette
   c. a place

MAIN IDEA

2. Another title for this story could possibly be ____.
   a. Luck Runs Out
   b. The Million Dollar Suitcase
   c. The Police Chief Mystery

DETAILS

3. Hasty and Blackie hid the suitcase_____
   _____.

SEQUENCE

4. After they bought a car, Hasty and Blackie _____
   _____.

FINDING PROOF

5. Mr. Rogers knew that Hasty and Blackie were crooks. Proof is that

_____ .

CAUSE AND EFFECT

6. The reason Hasty and Blackie pretended to be detectives is that

_____ .

WHAT DO YOU THINK?

What happened at the end of the story? Did the ending surprise you? What do you think happened to Hasty and Blackie? Why do you think the story is called "The Wrong House"? Do you think it's a good title?

NOTING SEQUENCE

The picture story below is a true story. But it is not in the right order. Number the frames from 1 to 4 to show the correct order or **sequence** of events.

He started to crawl through the air-conditioning ducts. ____

A prisoner decided to escape from a county jail. ____

And he landed in the courtroom below. ____

On his way, he fell through a weak spot in the ducts. ____

Here is another crime story with a strange "twist." But the lines are not in the right order. Decide which sentence should come first, which second, and so on. Number each sentence in the space in front of it.

_____ But he was too late, for the ax fell.

_____ The count remained silent.

_____ The queen forced the count to admit it, but he refused to tell who his helper was.

_____ So he was led to the chopping block.

_____ An English count and his helper stole the queen's jewels.

_____ "Tell me the name or you will be beheaded."

_____ As the ax came down, the count yelled, "OK, I'll talk!"

_____ The moral of this story: "Don't hatchet your counts before they chicken."

In reading, you should be able to put events or ideas into an order that makes sense. Read the sentences below. They are about events from the story "The Wrong House." Number the events to show the order in which they happened.

_____ Hasty and Blackie hid the suitcase.

_____ Blackie ran over a cop.

_____ They bought a new car.

_____ Hasty and Blackie stole a lot of money.

_____ They traveled east.

_____ Hasty thought of a plan.

_____ They found an empty house.

_____ Mr. Rogers ended their streak of luck.

_____ They found that the family had returned home.

VOCABULARY STUDY

annoy   dreadful   horrible   reflection
bathrobe   gasp   insurance   stain
collection harshly   invest

Write the words in the puzzle below. When you are done, you will see what a good detective must do.

a. a dirty spot   ☐ _ _ _ _

b. catch breath in shock   _ _ _ ☐

c. to bother; pester   _ _ _ ☐ _

d. what you put on
    after a bath   _ _ ☐ _ _ _ _ _

e. frightening or shocking   ☐ _ _ _ _ _ _ _

f. things gathered
    together   _ _ _ _ ☐ _ _ _ _ _

g. what you see in
    a mirror   _ _ _ _ _ _ ☐ _ _ _

h. policy that guards
    against loss   _ _ _ _ _ ☐ _ _ _

i. terrible; awful   _ _ _ _ ☐ _ _ _

j. said or done in
    rough way   _ _ _ _ _ ☐ _

k. spend money for
    future gain   _ _ _ _ ☐ _

THE PICASSO THIEF

What is a mystery? A case of a Who, a How, a When, a Where, and a Why.

In "The Picasso Thief," the What seems to be a stolen painting. Is it? As you read the mini-mystery, keep asking: Who? How? Where? When? and Why?

THE PICASSO THIEF by Julia Remine Piggin

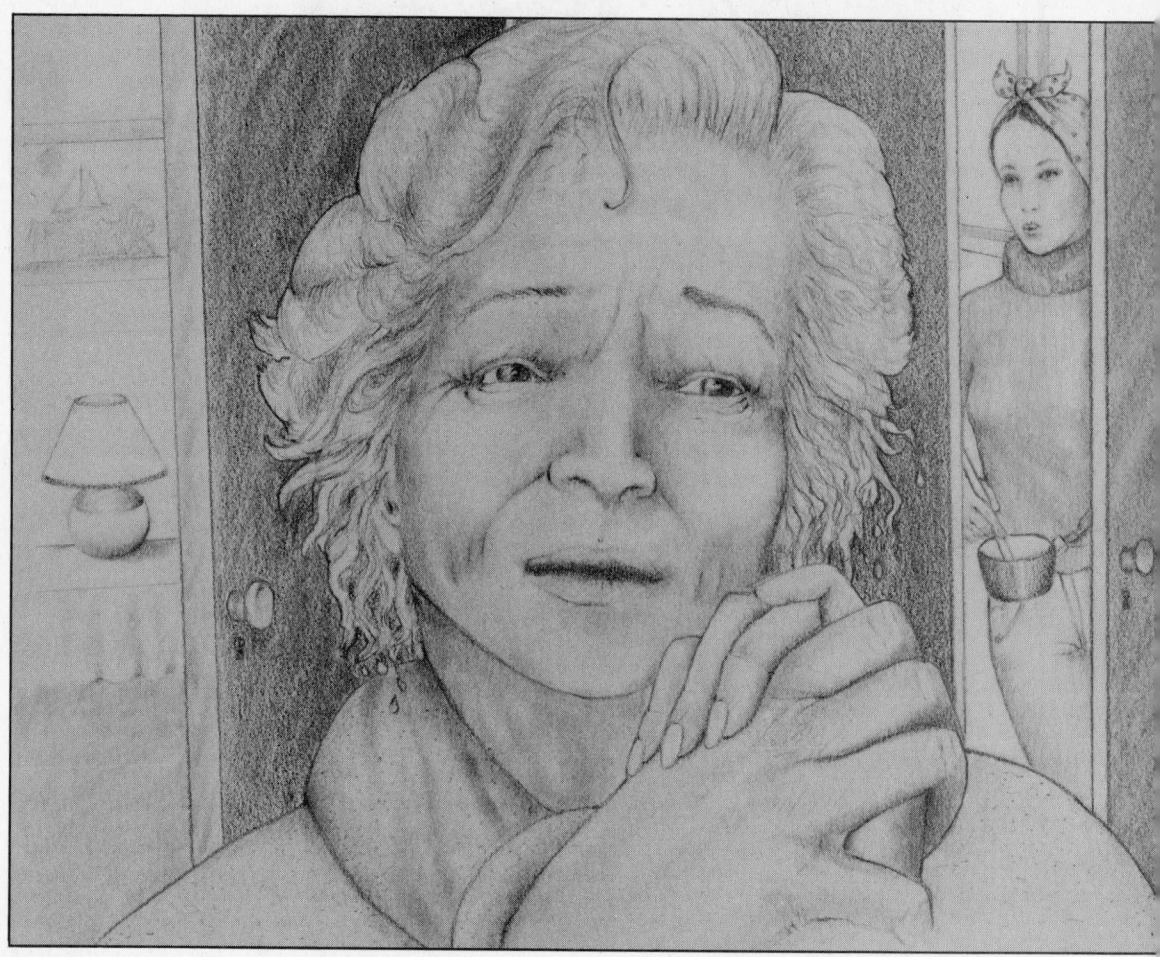

"Help! Help! Stop, thief! I've been robbed!" Sara Hull heard the cries and rushed into the hall outside her apartment.

Other doors opened, and neighbors peeked out. They saw Nella Parsony rushing up and down the hall. She was shouting and wringing her hands. Ms. Parsony's graying hair was damp. Her bare feet stuck out from under a blue bathrobe that showed damp stains. Sara ran to her.

"Please tell us what happened, Ms. Parsony," Sara said.

"Oh, it was horrible!" Ms. Parsony cried. "That dreadful face! He took my painting by Picasso, and maybe others as well. I haven't had time to check!"

The neighbors gasped. Ms. Parsony

had invested a fortune in her art collection.

"Oh, if only I hadn't left my bedroom window open," Ms. Parsony went on. "I never do, but this time...oh, his face!"

"Try to calm down," Sara Hull said. "And start at the beginning."

"I was in the bathroom taking a hot shower," Ms. Parsony explained.

"That's why I didn't hear him. I had the door shut and the window too. I turned off the shower and stepped out. I put on my robe — this one. I was standing at the sink when the door flew open and there he was!

"I was too scared to turn around, but I saw his face in the mirror. He had an awful look in his eyes. I thought he was going to kill me! But

then he laughed and slammed the door real hard. I couldn't get it open for a minute or two.

"When I got out, I looked at the wall. That's when I saw that my Picasso was gone. Oh, I'll have to see what else he took. I suppose — oh, somebody call the police."

Mr. Smith looked very concerned. "Sara, shouldn't you call your friend, that detective?" he asked. "Maybe if we act right away, they could catch this man."

"Come to my apartment," Sara told Ms. Parsony. "And we'll see what we can do." She took the crying woman by the arm and led her to the door.

Inside, Sara pushed Ms. Parsony into a chair. "Pull yourself together," she said harshly. "If you needed money, couldn't you have sold the painting? Or did you and your partner plan to do that too—*after* you collected the insurance money?"

"Whatever do you mean?" Ms. Parsony asked in an annoyed voice.

"You couldn't have seen a man's reflection in the mirror," Sara explained. "You said you had just stepped out of a hot shower in a closed room. In that case, the mirror would have been steamed over."

NOTING DETAILS

"In real life the crime comes first, then the search for clues," says author Julia Piggin. "But I start with a clue and then I dream up a crime to go with it."

Ms. Piggin wrote the story "The Picasso Thief." In that story, the clue is Ms. Parsony's remark about the bathroom mirror.

Once Ms. Piggin has a clue, she then decides who will be in her story (the characters) and what will happen (the action).

How did she do it? Fill in the details of her story outline that follows.

"The Picasso Thief"

A. The Clue: _____

B. The Characters

   1. Name of detective (or whoever solves the crime): _____

_____

   2. Victim (person or company): _____

   3. Criminal's Name: _____

C. The Action

1. What kind of crime was committed? _____

_____

2. What was the motive or reason? _____

_____

3. How was the crime committed? _____

_____

4. Where was it committed? _____

_____

5. How did the detective get involved? _____

_____

6. How was the clue discovered? _____

_____

_____

_____

_____

_____

WRITING ACTIVITY

Want to write your own mystery? Decide on a clue first. Here are some you might use:

- **A woman who claims she is deaf raises her voice when the radio is on.**

- **A man needing an alibi for Washington's Birthday says he spoke to a mail carrier. (There are no mail deliveries that day.)**

- **A man claims he hasn't talked with his mother for many years. Yet he knows she owns a puppy.**

- **A comb is found on the dresser of a totally bald man.**

Before you write your story, fill in an outline with your "idea starters."

A. The Clue

Your story will be built around the clue. What will it be? _____

_____

B. The Characters

Who will be in your story? Write the names of your main characters.

Detective: _____

Victim's Name: _____

Criminal's Name: _____

As you write your story, you will want to add other characters.

C. The Action

What will happen in your story? You can get started by answering these questions. (You may want to change some of your answers after you start writing your story.)

What kind of crime was committed? _____

_____

What was the motive? _____

_____

How was the crime committed? _____

_____

Where was it committed? _____

_____

How did the detective get involved? _____

_____

How was the clue discovered? _____

_____

Now you're ready to write. The clue may be the most important detail of your story. But don't give it away too soon. Save it for the end. That will help build suspense.

You could start your story with the crime itself. Then you can tell how the detective gets involved. Describe what the detective sees, including the clue.

When you've stated all the facts, reveal the surprise ending. Your detective can say that he or she knows who the criminal is. The detective can then reveal the clue, and tell how the crime was solved.

MID-BOOK ACTIVITY

You've just read five stories. Suppose the characters from those stories could meet each other. What do you think they might say? Imagine a room with the following people:

Brian (No Fat Chance)
Jenny (Picture of a Soldier)
Mr. Rogers (The Wrong House)
Sara Hull (The Picasso Thief)
Pete (Keeping Cool)
Tom (Picture of a Soldier)
Ms. Parsony (The Picasso Thief)
Hasty Hogan and **Blackie Burns** (The Wrong House)
Mercy (No Fat Chance)

Here are six bits of conversation. Decide which person might say each one. Then decide whom that person would be talking to. Under each conversation, write the name of the speaker. Then write the name of the person spoken to.

"Hey, you're cute. I said I was swearing off women, but I hear you just broke up with some guy in the Army. Doing anything tomorrow night?"

Speaker: _____

Speaking to: _____

"Lady, you're quite a detective. You figured out who stole that painting in no time. How about a regular job on the police force in my town? I can fix it up."

Speaker: _____

Speaking to: _____

"I know your face. Some girl came into the diner where I used to work and was showing your picture around. When are you two getting married?"

Speaking: _____

Speaking to: _____

"You men got in hot water because you didn't know who you were talking to. I got into hot water because I didn't know enough about hot water!"

Speaker: _____

Speaking to: _____

"I'm sorry you lost your job at the diner. But maybe you'll lose some weight, too, and be thin enough to go out with me."

Speaker: _____

Speaking to: _____

"Are you the chief of police? Can you have a girl arrested for going around saying you're in love with her when you haven't even met her?"

Speaker: _____

Speaking to: _____

VOCABULARY STUDY

basketball	fame	poster
calm	genie	unsure
exercise	impulse	you're

Some of these words are not pronounced the way they are spelled. For example:

Write the word that has a silent *l*. _____

Write the word that has a *g* that sounds like a *j*. _____

Write the word that has an *s* that sounds like a *z*. _____

Write the word that has an *s* that sounds like *sh*. _____

Write the words that belong in the puzzle below. When you are done, you'll have a clue to the kind of story you will be reading.

a. state of being
   well-known   □ _ _ _

b. a kind of sport   _ □ _ _ _ _ _ _ _ _

c. not sure   _ □ _ _ _ _

d. sign or picture   _ _ _ □ _ _ _

e. quiet and still   _ □ _ _

f. sudden desire to
   do something   _ _ _ _ _ □ _

g. short for *you are*   □ _ _ ' _ _

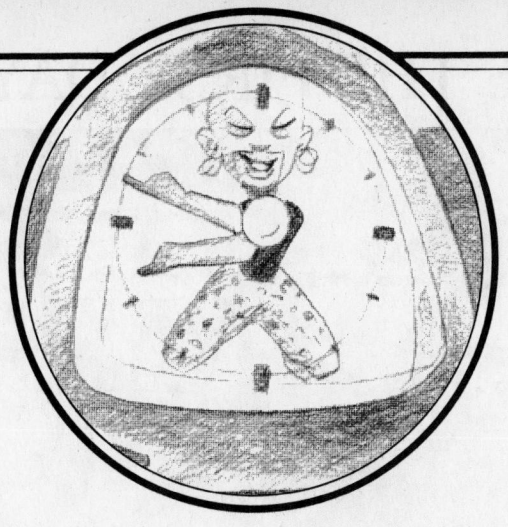

TODAY IS THE FIRST DAY OF...

If you could have one wish, what would it be for? Money? Fame? World peace?

As you read the story, think what you would do if you were in Robbie's place. Then be glad you're not!

TODAY IS THE FIRST DAY OF…

Robbie bought the poster on an impulse. It had a big yellow sun. "Today Is the First Day of the Rest of Your Life!" was printed over the sun.

Tomorrow Robbie would make a fresh start. He'd do some exercises. He'd get in shape for basketball. If only he had his own clock. Then he would be able to get up early.

Robbie spotted the clock in an old store window. A picture of a desert was painted on the clock's face. A genie with a strange smile was sitting in the sand. His arms were the hands of the clock.

Robbie walked into the store.

"Can I help you?" an old man asked.

"Yes. That clock in the window —" Robbie said. "How much is it?"

The old man walked over to the window. "*That* one? One dollar!" he said quickly.

"A dollar?" The look of surprise must have showed on Robbie's face. But the old man did not understand it.

"OK," the man said. "Fifty cents."

"Fifty cents?" It seemed impossible. "Does it work?" Robbie asked.

by James Shannon

"Very well," the man said. "How about a quarter?"

"A quarter?" Robbie reached into his pocket.

"Never mind," the old man said. "You look like you need a clock like this. Here, take it!"

Robbie took the clock and left the store. Why had the man given it to him for nothing? He was all mixed up.

That night, the clock started to hum. Robbie took a close look. He was sure the genie's eyes had been open when he bought the clock. Now they were closed. "I must have been wrong about the eyes," Robbie told himself as he dropped off to sleep.

When Robbie woke up, the first thing he saw was "Today Is the First Day of the Rest of Your Life!" Then he heard the hum and knew what woke him. The genie's arms pointed to 5:30. His smile made Robbie think of something. Robbie jumped out of bed. He did push-ups and knee-bends. He was ready to take on a whole new life.

People saw the change in Robbie right away. He felt smart in all his classes. In gym, he played basketball better than ever before. "Take it easy," the coach had told him. "We want to save some of that for the season." Robbie was almost sure he had made the team.

After school, Mary Beth Carpenter asked if he was going to the dance. Robbie had liked Mary Beth for two years. But he'd never been able to do anything about it before. Now he said, "Well, I thought about it. Of course, I don't know who to ask —"

Robbie watched her bite her lip. He felt cool and calm. Finally he said, "Want to go with me?"

"Yes, I'd like that," Mary said.

"Good," Robbie said as he headed toward his locker. "I'll see you tomorrow."

By the time Robbie got home, his whole life had changed. He was going to be on the basketball team. He had a date with Mary Beth. He went to his room, whistling to himself. It felt good to be a "new" man.

The poster still hung on the wall. The clock still hummed. After a while, Robbie looked at the clock. The genie's eyes were open! He was sure they had been closed the night before. And that smile! It seemed to be making fun of him.

Robbie threw the clock against the wall. The humming stopped. The glass cover fell off.

"You didn't need to do that, you know."

Robbie looked around the room. Where was the voice coming from? Then he spotted a little man sitting in the corner. His legs were folded under him. His arms were crossed on his chest.

Robbie looked again.

"Oh, I'm here, all right. But all you had to do was rub the clock a few times. Haven't you read the books? Do you think we only come in lamps?"

"You can't be the —" Robbie stopped.

"But of course I can," the man said with a smile. "I *am*."

Robbie sat back and wondered. Was this why the storekeeper had been so happy to get rid of the clock?

"Yes, that's true," the genie said. It was as if he knew Robbie's thoughts. "Mr. Hoffman and I never got along very well."

"Does this mean you're going to stay here?" Robbie asked.

"Only until you make a wish." The genie clapped his hands together. "Then I'll be on my way."

Robbie began to think of all the things he had ever wanted. After a day like today, there wasn't much else to ask for. He'd like to have more

days like today. But you never know what a day will bring.

"You *could* know what a day is going to be like if you wanted to," the genie said, reading his mind. "I could tell you just what tomorrow would be like."

Tomorrow could never be as good as today, Robbie thought.

"True," the genie said. "Today was a good one for you."

"That's it!" Robbie said at last. "How about living today over again?"

"You could, I suppose," the genie said. "But no one has ever asked for that before. Most people ask for money or fame."

"Nope, that's my wish," Robbie said. "I want to live today over again, just as it happened. And I want to know what's going to happen."

The genie smiled. He seemed a little unsure for a moment. Then he snapped his fingers.

When Robbie woke, the first thing he saw was "Today Is the First Day of the Rest of Your Life!" Then he heard the hum and knew what woke him. The genie's arms pointed to 5:30. His smile made Robbie think of something.

The wish! He was going to live the day over again. He jumped out of bed and started doing push-ups and knee-bends. He remembered how many he

had done the day before. He tried to do one more. But he found himself getting dressed instead.

His school day was just the same. But now Robbie noticed things he had not seen the day before. Before gym, he overheard Billy Johnson telling someone that he was sick. But he was going to try to make the team just the same. Robbie remembered how poorly Billy had played. He had been able to steal the ball from Billy three times. Yesterday, Robbie had forgotten that Billy had not felt well.

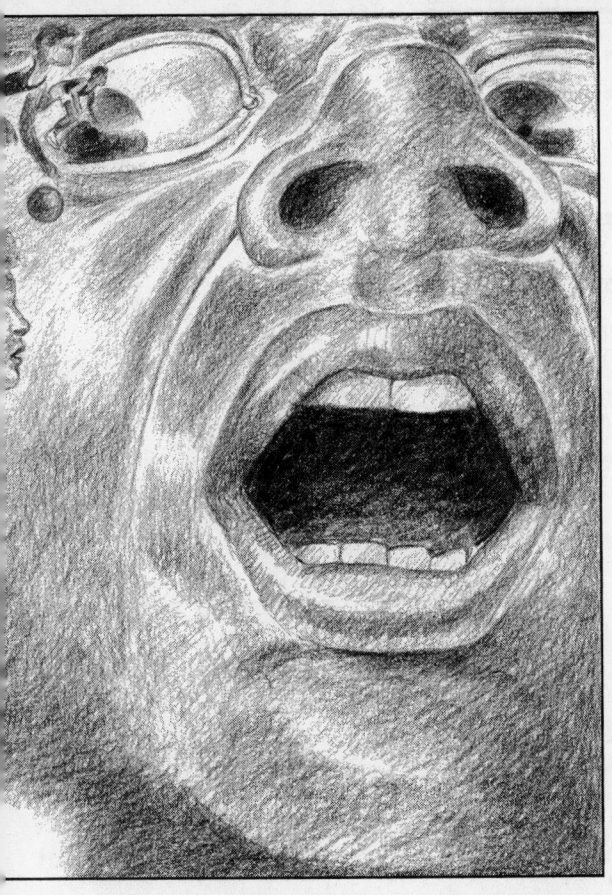

Robbie didn't want to make Billy look bad in the game. But he couldn't help it. Then the coach came over and told Robbie to "save some of that for the season." Robbie saw that Billy looked ready to cry.

When Robbie met Mary Beth, he was surprised at how mean he had been to her. He knew he had been covering up his own feelings. But still, he was glad the day was almost over.

At home, Robbie picked up the clock to look at it. Then he threw it against the wall.

"You didn't need to do that, you know."

The genie was sitting in the corner. "Oh, I'm here, all right. But all you had to do was rub the clock a few times. Haven't you read the books? Do you think we only come in lamps?"

Robbie wanted to say, "I know. I know. We've been through all this before." But he could only say the same words as the day before.

When they got to the part about making a wish, Robbie began to worry. Wasn't it time to stop all of this? Wasn't it time for the genie to go on to someone else?

He began to really worry when he heard himself say, "Nope, that's my wish! I want to live today over again, just as it happened. And I want to know what's going to happen."

Robbie wanted to scream out, "No! Stop! That's enough!" But he was helpless as he saw the genie smile. And then the genie snapped his fingers.

When Robbie woke up, the first thing he saw was "Today Is the First Day of the Rest of Your Life!" Then he heard the hum and knew what woke him. The genie's arms pointed to 5:30. His smile made Robbie think of something. . . .

READING CHECK

WORD MEANING FROM CONTEXT

1. "It felt good to be a 'new' man." This means that _____ .
   a. Robbie changed places with someone
   b. Robbie felt that he had changed
   c. Robbie met someone new

MAIN IDEA

2. This story is about someone who _____

_____ .

DETAILS

3. List three good things that happened to Robbie after he bought the poster and clock.

   a. _____

   b. _____

   c. _____

SEQUENCE

4. Number these events to show the order that they happened in the story.

   _____ Robbie saw the clock in the store window.

   _____ Robbie realized that Billy was sick.

_____ Robbie was worried about the wish he had made.

_____ Robbie bought the poster.

_____ Robbie played basketball better than ever before.

FINDING PROOF

5. The coach thought that Robbie played well. Proof is that _____

_____ .

CAUSE AND EFFECT

6. The genie appeared when Robbie _____

_____ .

WHAT DO YOU THINK?

Some information in the story is not stated. But you can make guesses and draw conclusions from what *is* said. Read each statement below. Check the ones you think are true.

_____ Robbie will have a good time at the dance.

_____ Robbie will relive his day over and over again.

_____ The storekeeper will try to get the clock back.

_____ Robbie is sorry he made the wish.

_____ Robbie will have a chance to change his wish.

_____ The wish didn't turn out as Robbie expected.

Do you think this story could have really happened? Why or why not?

FOLLOWING DIRECTIONS

What does this joke have in common with the story "Today Is the First Day of ..."? In both, the boys are stuck with wishes they didn't quite expect. What's more, their wishes are *perpetual* — that is, they will last forever.

On the next few pages is a **perpetual calendar.** It will give you any date over a wide range of years. This one covers 1700 to 2108. You can look into the past and the future. You won't even need a genie. Just follow the directions—and you'll be set for 400 years!

HOW TO USE A PERPETUAL CALENDAR

On what day of the week were you born? Here's how to find out.

1. First, think of the year in which you were born. Then find that year in the tables on pages 86 and 87. Next to each year is a letter. Notice the letter that is next to the year you are looking up.

2. Next, look at the calendars on pages 88-91. Each calendar has a letter at the top. Find the calendar that has the same letter as the letter of your birth year.

3. Now look up your birthday on the lettered calendar. Then you can see on which day you were born.

> **Example:**
> Suppose you were born March 23, 1963. You'd find the year 1963 on the table. Next to 1963 is the letter C. Turn to calendar C and look for the month of March. Then look up March 23rd. You'll see that it was a Saturday.

Now check out your own birthday. On what day of the week were you born?_____

Here is an old rhyme. See what it says about people who are born on that day. Do you think the rhyme describes you?

MONDAY'S CHILD IS FAIR OF FACE
TUESDAY'S CHILD IS FULL OF GRACE
WEDNESDAY'S CHILD IS FULL OF WOE
THURSDAY'S CHILD HAS FAR TO GO
FRIDAY'S CHILD IS LOVING AND GIVING
SATURDAY'S CHILD HAS TO WORK FOR ITS LIVING
BUT A CHILD THAT'S BORN ON THE SABBATH DAY
   IS FAIR AND WISE, AND HAPPY — THEY SAY!

Now use the calendar to look into the past.

The Declaration of Independence was signed July 4, 1776. On what day of the week was that? _____

The first telephone talk was on January 25, 1915. On what day of the week did it fall? _____

World War I ended on November 11, 1918. What day was it?

_____

The first talking movie pictures were shown July 6, 1928. What day was it? _____

The first "Five and Ten" store opened February 22, 1879. What day was it? _____

A law lowering the voting age to 18 was passed on June 30, 1971. What day was it? _____

Now use the calendar to look into the future.

On what day of the week will your birthday be next year?

_____

How old will you be in the year 2001? On what day will your birthday

fall? _____

Write down the birthday of a good friend. _____

On what day will it fall next year? _____

On what day will July 4, 1994 fall? _____

Write down the date of a favorite holiday. _____

On what day will it fall in the year 2073? _____

On what day will April 1, 1984 fall? _____

TABLE OF YEARS

1700-1799

1700				N
1701	1729	1757	1785	I
1702	1730	1758	1786	J
1703	1731	1759	1787	K
1704	1732	1760	1788	L
1705	1733	1761	1789	M
1706	1734	1762	1790	N
1707	1735	1763	1791	I
1708	1736	1764	1792	A
1709	1737	1765	1793	C
1710	1738	1766	1794	G
1711	1739	1767	1795	M
1712	1740	1768	1796	E
1713	1741	1769	1797	J
1714	1742	1770	1798	K
1715	1743	1771	1799	C
1716	1744	1772		D
1717	1745	1773		N
1718	1746	1774		I
1719	1747	1775		J
1720	1748	1776		B
1721	1749	1777		G
1722	1750	1778		M
1723	1751	1779		N
1724	1752	1780		F
1725	1753	1781		K
1726	1754	1782		C
1727	1755	1783		G
1728	1756	1784		H

1800-1899

1800				G
1801	1829	1857	1885	M
1802	1830	1858	1886	N
1803	1831	1859	1887	I
1804	1832	1860	1888	A
1805	1833	1861	1889	C
1806	1834	1862	1890	G
1807	1835	1863	1891	M
1808	1836	1864	1892	E
1809	1837	1865	1893	J
1810	1838	1866	1894	K
1811	1839	1867	1895	C
1812	1840	1868	1896	D
1813	1841	1869	1897	N
1814	1842	1870	1898	I
1815	1843	1871	1899	J
1816	1844	1872		B
1817	1845	1873		G
1818	1846	1874		M
1819	1847	1875		N
1820	1848	1876		F
1821	1849	1877		K
1822	1850	1878		C
1823	1851	1879		G
1824	1852	1880		H
1825	1853	1881		I
1826	1854	1882		J
1827	1855	1883		K
1828	1856	1884		L

1900-2012

1900				**K**
1901	1929	1957	1985	**C**
1902	1930	1958	1986	**G**
1903	1931	1959	1987	**M**
1904	1932	1960	1988	**E**
1905	1933	1961	1989	**J**
1906	1934	1962	1990	**K**
1907	1935	1963	1991	**C**
1908	1936	1964	1992	**D**
1909	1937	1965	1993	**N**
1910	1938	1966	1994	**I**
1911	1939	1967	1995	**J**
1912	1940	1968	1996	**B**
1913	1941	1969	1997	**G**
1914	1942	1970	1998	**M**
1915	1943	1971	1999	**N**
1916	1944	1972	2000	**F**
1917	1945	1973	2001	**K**
1918	1946	1974	2002	**C**
1919	1947	1975	2003	**G**
1920	1948	1976	2004	**H**
1921	1949	1977	2005	**I**
1922	1950	1978	2006	**J**
1923	1951	1979	2007	**K**
1924	1952	1980	2008	**L**
1925	1953	1981	2009	**M**
1926	1954	1982	2010	**N**
1927	1955	1983	2011	**I**
1928	1956	1984	2012	**A**

2013-2108

				K
2013	2041	2069	2097	**C**
2014	2042	2070	2098	**G**
2015	2043	2071	2099	**M**
2016	2044	2072		**E**
2017	2045	2073		**J**
2018	2046	2074		**K**
2019	2047	2075		**C**
2020	2048	2076		**D**
2021	2049	2077	2100	**N**
2022	2050	2078		**I**
2023	2051	2079		**J**
2024	2052	2080		**B**
2025	2053	2081		**G**
2026	2054	2082		**M**
2027	2055	2083		**N**
2028	2056	2084		**F**
2029	2057	2085		**K**
2030	2058	2086		**C**
2031	2059	2087		**G**
2032	2060	2088		**H**
2033	2061	2089	2101	**I**
2034	2062	2090	2102	**J**
2035	2063	2091	2103	**K**
2036	2064	2092	2104	**L**
2037	2065	2093	2105	**M**
2038	2066	2094	2106	**N**
2039	2067	2095	2107	**I**
2040	2068	2096	2108	**A**

CALENDARS

A

JANUARY
```
S  M  T  W  T  F  S
 1  2  3  4  5  6  7
 8  9 10 11 12 13 14
15 16 17 18 19 20 21
22 23 24 25 26 27 28
29 30 31
```

FEBRUARY
```
S  M  T  W  T  F  S
             1  2  3  4
 5  6  7  8  9 10 11
12 13 14 15 16 17 18
19 20 21 22 23 24 25
26 27 28 29
```

MARCH
```
S  M  T  W  T  F  S
             1  2  3
 4  5  6  7  8  9 10
11 12 13 14 15 16 17
18 19 20 21 22 23 24
25 26 27 28 29 30 31
```

APRIL
```
S  M  T  W  T  F  S
 1  2  3  4  5  6  7
 8  9 10 11 12 13 14
15 16 17 18 19 20 21
22 23 24 25 26 27 28
29 30
```

MAY
```
S  M  T  W  T  F  S
       1  2  3  4  5
 6  7  8  9 10 11 12
13 14 15 16 17 18 19
20 21 22 23 24 25 26
27 28 29 30 31
```

JUNE
```
S  M  T  W  T  F  S
                1  2
 3  4  5  6  7  8  9
10 11 12 13 14 15 16
17 18 19 20 21 22 23
24 25 26 27 28 29 30
```

JULY
```
S  M  T  W  T  F  S
 1  2  3  4  5  6  7
 8  9 10 11 12 13 14
15 16 17 18 19 20 21
22 23 24 25 26 27 28
29 30 31
```

AUGUST
```
S  M  T  W  T  F  S
             1  2  3  4
 5  6  7  8  9 10 11
12 13 14 15 16 17 18
19 20 21 22 23 24 25
26 27 28 29 30 31
```

SEPTEMBER
```
S  M  T  W  T  F  S
                   1
 2  3  4  5  6  7  8
 9 10 11 12 13 14 15
16 17 18 19 20 21 22
23 24 25 26 27 28 29
30
```

OCTOBER
```
S  M  T  W  T  F  S
    1  2  3  4  5  6
 7  8  9 10 11 12 13
14 15 16 17 18 19 20
21 22 23 24 25 26 27
28 29 30 31
```

NOVEMBER
```
S  M  T  W  T  F  S
          1  2  3
 4  5  6  7  8  9 10
11 12 13 14 15 16 17
18 19 20 21 22 23 24
25 26 27 28 29 30
```

DECEMBER
```
S  M  T  W  T  F  S
                   1
 2  3  4  5  6  7  8
 9 10 11 12 13 14 15
16 17 18 19 20 21 22
23 24 25 26 27 28 29
30 31
```

B

JANUARY
```
S  M  T  W  T  F  S
    1  2  3  4  5  6
 7  8  9 10 11 12 13
14 15 16 17 18 19 20
21 22 23 24 25 26 27
28 29 30 31
```

FEBRUARY
```
S  M  T  W  T  F  S
          1  2  3
 4  5  6  7  8  9 10
11 12 13 14 15 16 17
18 19 20 21 22 23 24
25 26 27 28 29
```

MARCH
```
S  M  T  W  T  F  S
                1  2
 3  4  5  6  7  8  9
10 11 12 13 14 15 16
17 18 19 20 21 22 23
24 25 26 27 28 29 30
31
```

APRIL
```
S  M  T  W  T  F  S
    1  2  3  4  5  6
 7  8  9 10 11 12 13
14 15 16 17 18 19 20
21 22 23 24 25 26 27
28 29 30
```

MAY
```
S  M  T  W  T  F  S
             1  2  3  4
 5  6  7  8  9 10 11
12 13 14 15 16 17 18
19 20 21 22 23 24 25
26 27 28 29 30 31
```

JUNE
```
S  M  T  W  T  F  S
                   1
 2  3  4  5  6  7  8
 9 10 11 12 13 14 15
16 17 18 19 20 21 22
23 24 25 26 27 28 29
30
```

JULY
```
S  M  T  W  T  F  S
    1  2  3  4  5  6
 7  8  9 10 11 12 13
14 15 16 17 18 19 20
21 22 23 24 25 26 27
28 29 30 31
```

AUGUST
```
S  M  T  W  T  F  S
          1  2  3
 4  5  6  7  8  9 10
11 12 13 14 15 16 17
18 19 20 21 22 23 24
25 26 27 28 29 30 31
```

SEPTEMBER
```
S  M  T  W  T  F  S
 1  2  3  4  5  6  7
 8  9 10 11 12 13 14
15 16 17 18 19 20 21
22 23 24 25 26 27 28
29 30
```

OCTOBER
```
S  M  T  W  T  F  S
       1  2  3  4  5
 6  7  8  9 10 11 12
13 14 15 16 17 18 19
20 21 22 23 24 25 26
27 28 29 30 31
```

NOVEMBER
```
S  M  T  W  T  F  S
                1  2
 3  4  5  6  7  8  9
10 11 12 13 14 15 16
17 18 19 20 21 22 23
24 25 26 27 28 29 30
```

DECEMBER
```
S  M  T  W  T  F  S
                   1
 2  3  4  5  6  7  8
 9 10 11 12 13 14 15
16 17 18 19 20 21 22
23 24 25 26 27 28 29
30 31
```

C

JANUARY

S	M	T	W	T	F	S
		1	2	3	4	5
6	7	8	9	10	11	12
13	14	15	16	17	18	19
20	21	22	23	24	25	26
27	28	29	30	31		

FEBRUARY

S	M	T	W	T	F	S
					1	2
3	4	5	6	7	8	9
10	11	12	13	14	15	16
17	18	19	20	21	22	23
24	25	26	27	28		

MARCH

S	M	T	W	T	F	S
					1	2
3	4	5	6	7	8	9
10	11	12	13	14	15	16
17	18	19	20	21	22	23
24	25	26	27	28	29	30
31						

APRIL

S	M	T	W	T	F	S
	1	2	3	4	5	6
7	8	9	10	11	12	13
14	15	16	17	18	19	20
21	22	23	24	25	26	27
28	29	30				

MAY

S	M	T	W	T	F	S
			1	2	3	4
5	6	7	8	9	10	11
12	13	14	15	16	17	18
19	20	21	22	23	24	25
26	27	28	29	30	31	

JUNE

S	M	T	W	T	F	S
						1
2	3	4	5	6	7	8
9	10	11	12	13	14	15
16	17	18	19	20	21	22
23	24	25	26	27	28	29
30						

JULY

S	M	T	W	T	F	S
	1	2	3	4	5	6
7	8	9	10	11	12	13
14	15	16	17	18	19	20
21	22	23	24	25	26	27
28	29	30	31			

AUGUST

S	M	T	W	T	F	S
				1	2	3
4	5	6	7	8	9	10
11	12	13	14	15	16	17
18	19	20	21	22	23	24
25	26	27	28	29	30	31

SEPTEMBER

S	M	T	W	T	F	S
1	2	3	4	5	6	7
8	9	10	11	12	13	14
15	16	17	18	19	20	21
22	23	24	25	26	27	28
29	30					

OCTOBER

S	M	T	W	T	F	S
		1	2	3	4	5
6	7	8	9	10	11	12
13	14	15	16	17	18	19
20	21	22	23	24	25	26
27	28	29	30	31		

NOVEMBER

S	M	T	W	T	F	S
					1	2
3	4	5	6	7	8	9
10	11	12	13	14	15	16
17	18	19	20	21	22	23
24	25	26	27	28	29	30

DECEMBER

S	M	T	W	T	F	S
1	2	3	4	5	6	7
8	9	10	11	12	13	14
15	16	17	18	19	20	21
22	23	24	25	26	27	28
29	30	31				

D

JANUARY

S	M	T	W	T	F	S
			1	2	3	4
5	6	7	8	9	10	11
12	13	14	15	16	17	18
19	20	21	22	23	24	25
26	27	28	29	30	31	

FEBRUARY

S	M	T	W	T	F	S
						1
2	3	4	5	6	7	8
9	10	11	12	13	14	15
16	17	18	19	20	21	22
23	24	25	26	27	28	29

MARCH

S	M	T	W	T	F	S
1	2	3	4	5	6	7
8	9	10	11	12	13	14
15	16	17	18	19	20	21
22	23	24	25	26	27	28
29	30	31				

APRIL

S	M	T	W	T	F	S
			1	2	3	4
5	6	7	8	9	10	11
12	13	14	15	16	17	18
19	20	21	22	23	24	25
26	27	28	29	30		

MAY

S	M	T	W	T	F	S
					1	2
3	4	5	6	7	8	9
10	11	12	13	14	15	16
17	18	19	20	21	22	23
24	25	26	27	28	29	30
31						

JUNE

S	M	T	W	T	F	S
	1	2	3	4	5	6
7	8	9	10	11	12	13
14	15	16	17	18	19	20
21	22	23	24	25	26	27
28	29	30				

JULY

S	M	T	W	T	F	S
			1	2	3	4
5	6	7	8	9	10	11
12	13	14	15	16	17	18
19	20	21	22	23	24	25
26	27	28	29	30	31	

AUGUST

S	M	T	W	T	F	S
						1
2	3	4	5	6	7	8
9	10	11	12	13	14	15
16	17	18	19	20	21	22
23	24	25	26	27	28	29
30	31					

SEPTEMBER

S	M	T	W	T	F	S
		1	2	3	4	5
6	7	8	9	10	11	12
13	14	15	16	17	18	19
20	21	22	23	24	25	26
27	28	29	30			

OCTOBER

S	M	T	W	T	F	S
				1	2	3
4	5	6	7	8	9	10
11	12	13	14	15	16	17
18	19	20	21	22	23	24
25	26	27	28	29	30	31

NOVEMBER

S	M	T	W	T	F	S
1	2	3	4	5	6	7
8	9	10	11	12	13	14
15	16	17	18	19	20	21
22	23	24	25	26	27	28
29	30					

DECEMBER

S	M	T	W	T	F	S
		1	2	3	4	5
6	7	8	9	10	11	12
13	14	15	16	17	18	19
20	21	22	23	24	25	26
27	28	29	30	31		

E

JANUARY

S	M	T	W	T	F	S
					1	2
3	4	5	6	7	8	9
10	11	12	13	14	15	16
17	18	19	20	21	22	23
24	25	26	27	28	29	30
31						

FEBRUARY

S	M	T	W	T	F	S
	1	2	3	4	5	6
7	8	9	10	11	12	13
14	15	16	17	18	19	20
21	22	23	24	25	26	27
28	29					

MARCH

S	M	T	W	T	F	S
		1	2	3	4	5
6	7	8	9	10	11	12
13	14	15	16	17	18	19
20	21	22	23	24	25	26
27	28	29	30	31		

APRIL

S	M	T	W	T	F	S
					1	2
3	4	5	6	7	8	9
10	11	12	13	14	15	16
17	18	19	20	21	22	23
24	25	26	27	28	29	30

MAY

S	M	T	W	T	F	S
1	2	3	4	5	6	7
8	9	10	11	12	13	14
15	16	17	18	19	20	21
22	23	24	25	26	27	28
29	30	31				

JUNE

S	M	T	W	T	F	S
			1	2	3	4
5	6	7	8	9	10	11
12	13	14	15	16	17	18
19	20	21	22	23	24	25
26	27	28	29	30		

JULY

S	M	T	W	T	F	S
					1	2
3	4	5	6	7	8	9
10	11	12	13	14	15	16
17	18	19	20	21	22	23
24	25	26	27	28	29	30
31						

AUGUST

S	M	T	W	T	F	S
	1	2	3	4	5	6
7	8	9	10	11	12	13
14	15	16	17	18	19	20
21	22	23	24	25	26	27
28	29	30	31			

SEPTEMBER

S	M	T	W	T	F	S
				1	2	3
4	5	6	7	8	9	10
11	12	13	14	15	16	17
18	19	20	21	22	23	24
25	26	27	28	29	30	

OCTOBER

S	M	T	W	T	F	S
						1
2	3	4	5	6	7	8
9	10	11	12	13	14	15
16	17	18	19	20	21	22
23	24	25	26	27	28	29
30	31					

NOVEMBER

S	M	T	W	T	F	S
		1	2	3	4	5
6	7	8	9	10	11	12
13	14	15	16	17	18	19
20	21	22	23	24	25	26
27	28	29	30			

DECEMBER

S	M	T	W	T	F	S
				1	2	3
4	5	6	7	8	9	10
11	12	13	14	15	16	17
18	19	20	21	22	23	24
25	26	27	28	29	30	31

F

JANUARY

S	M	T	W	T	F	S
						1
2	3	4	5	6	7	8
9	10	11	12	13	14	15
16	17	18	19	20	21	22
23	24	25	26	27	28	29
30	31					

FEBRUARY

S	M	T	W	T	F	S
		1	2	3	4	5
6	7	8	9	10	11	12
13	14	15	16	17	18	19
20	21	22	23	24	25	26
27	28	29				

MARCH

S	M	T	W	T	F	S
			1	2	3	4
5	6	7	8	9	10	11
12	13	14	15	16	17	18
19	20	21	22	23	24	25
26	27	28	29	30	31	

APRIL

S	M	T	W	T	F	S
						1
2	3	4	5	6	7	8
9	10	11	12	13	14	15
16	17	18	19	20	21	22
23	24	25	26	27	28	29
30						

MAY

S	M	T	W	T	F	S
	1	2	3	4	5	6
7	8	9	10	11	12	13
14	15	16	17	18	19	20
21	22	23	24	25	26	27
28	29	30	31			

JUNE

S	M	T	W	T	F	S
				1	2	3
4	5	6	7	8	9	10
11	12	13	14	15	16	17
18	19	20	21	22	23	24
25	26	27	28	29	30	

JULY

S	M	T	W	T	F	S
						1
2	3	4	5	6	7	8
9	10	11	12	13	14	15
16	17	18	19	20	21	22
23	24	25	26	27	28	29
30	31					

AUGUST

S	M	T	W	T	F	S
		1	2	3	4	5
6	7	8	9	10	11	12
13	14	15	16	17	18	19
20	21	22	23	24	25	26
27	28	29	30	31		

SEPTEMBER

S	M	T	W	T	F	S
					1	2
3	4	5	6	7	8	9
10	11	12	13	14	15	16
17	18	19	20	21	22	23
24	25	26	27	28	29	30

OCTOBER

S	M	T	W	T	F	S
1	2	3	4	5	6	7
8	9	10	11	12	13	14
15	16	17	18	19	20	21
22	23	24	25	26	27	28
29	30	31				

NOVEMBER

S	M	T	W	T	F	S
			1	2	3	4
5	6	7	8	9	10	11
12	13	14	15	16	17	18
19	20	21	22	23	24	25
26	27	28	29	30		

DECEMBER

S	M	T	W	T	F	S
					1	2
3	4	5	6	7	8	9
10	11	12	13	14	15	16
17	18	19	20	21	22	23
24	25	26	27	28	29	30
31						

G

```
        JANUARY                  FEBRUARY                  MARCH
S  M  T  W  T  F  S       S  M  T  W  T  F  S       S  M  T  W  T  F  S
         1  2  3  4                         1                         1
5  6  7  8  9 10 11       2  3  4  5  6  7  8       2  3  4  5  6  7  8
12 13 14 15 16 17 18      9 10 11 12 13 14 15       9 10 11 12 13 14 15
19 20 21 22 23 24 25     16 17 18 19 20 21 22      16 17 18 19 20 21 22
26 27 28 29 30 31        23 24 25 26 27 28         23 24 25 26 27 28 29
                                                   30 31

         APRIL                     MAY                      JUNE
S  M  T  W  T  F  S       S  M  T  W  T  F  S       S  M  T  W  T  F  S
         1  2  3  4  5                1  2  3       1  2  3  4  5  6  7
6  7  8  9 10 11 12       4  5  6  7  8  9 10       8  9 10 11 12 13 14
13 14 15 16 17 18 19     11 12 13 14 15 16 17      15 16 17 18 19 20 21
20 21 22 23 24 25 26     18 19 20 21 22 23 24      22 23 24 25 26 27 28
27 28 29 30              25 26 27 28 29 30 31      29 30

         JULY                    AUGUST                  SEPTEMBER
S  M  T  W  T  F  S       S  M  T  W  T  F  S       S  M  T  W  T  F  S
         1  2  3  4  5                   1  2       1  2  3  4  5  6
6  7  8  9 10 11 12       3  4  5  6  7  8  9       7  8  9 10 11 12 13
13 14 15 16 17 18 19     10 11 12 13 14 15 16      14 15 16 17 18 19 20
20 21 22 23 24 25 26     17 18 19 20 21 22 23      21 22 23 24 25 26 27
27 28 29 30 31           24 25 26 27 28 29 30      28 29 30
                         31

        OCTOBER                  NOVEMBER                 DECEMBER
S  M  T  W  T  F  S       S  M  T  W  T  F  S       S  M  T  W  T  F  S
            1  2  3  4                         1       1  2  3  4  5  6
5  6  7  8  9 10 11       2  3  4  5  6  7  8       7  8  9 10 11 12 13
12 13 14 15 16 17 18      9 10 11 12 13 14 15      14 15 16 17 18 19 20
19 20 21 22 23 24 25     16 17 18 19 20 21 22      21 22 23 24 25 26 27
26 27 28 29 30 31        23 24 25 26 27 28 29      28 29 30 31
                         30
```

H

```
        JANUARY                  FEBRUARY                  MARCH
S  M  T  W  T  F  S       S  M  T  W  T  F  S       S  M  T  W  T  F  S
            1  2  3       1  2  3  4  5  6  7          1  2  3  4  5  6
4  5  6  7  8  9 10       8  9 10 11 12 13 14       7  8  9 10 11 12 13
11 12 13 14 15 16 17     15 16 17 18 19 20 21      14 15 16 17 18 19 20
18 19 20 21 22 23 24     22 23 24 25 26 27 28      21 22 23 24 25 26 27
25 26 27 28 29 30 31     29                        28 29 30 31

         APRIL                     MAY                      JUNE
S  M  T  W  T  F  S       S  M  T  W  T  F  S       S  M  T  W  T  F  S
            1  2  3                         1                1  2  3  4  5
4  5  6  7  8  9 10       2  3  4  5  6  7  8       6  7  8  9 10 11 12
11 12 13 14 15 16 17      9 10 11 12 13 14 15      13 14 15 16 17 18 19
18 19 20 21 22 23 24     16 17 18 19 20 21 22      20 21 22 23 24 25 26
25 26 27 28 29 30        23 24 25 26 27 28 29      27 28 29 30
                         30 31

         JULY                    AUGUST                  SEPTEMBER
S  M  T  W  T  F  S       S  M  T  W  T  F  S       S  M  T  W  T  F  S
            1  2  3       1  2  3  4  5  6  7                1  2  3  4
4  5  6  7  8  9 10       8  9 10 11 12 13 14       5  6  7  8  9 10 11
11 12 13 14 15 16 17     15 16 17 18 19 20 21      12 13 14 15 16 17 18
18 19 20 21 22 23 24     22 23 24 25 26 27 28      19 20 21 22 23 24 25
25 26 27 28 29 30 31     29 30 31                  26 27 28 29 30

        OCTOBER                  NOVEMBER                 DECEMBER
S  M  T  W  T  F  S       S  M  T  W  T  F  S       S  M  T  W  T  F  S
               1  2             1  2  3  4  5  6                1  2  3  4
3  4  5  6  7  8  9       7  8  9 10 11 12 13       5  6  7  8  9 10 11
10 11 12 13 14 15 16     14 15 16 17 18 19 20      12 13 14 15 16 17 18
17 18 19 20 21 22 23     21 22 23 24 25 26 27      19 20 21 22 23 24 25
24 25 26 27 28 29 30     28 29 30                  26 27 28 29 30 31
31
```

I

```
        JANUARY                  FEBRUARY                  MARCH
S  M  T  W  T  F  S       S  M  T  W  T  F  S       S  M  T  W  T  F  S
                  1             1  2  3  4  5             1  2  3  4  5
2  3  4  5  6  7  8       6  7  8  9 10 11 12       6  7  8  9 10 11 12
9 10 11 12 13 14 15      13 14 15 16 17 18 19      13 14 15 16 17 18 19
16 17 18 19 20 21 22     20 21 22 23 24 25 26      20 21 22 23 24 25 26
23 24 25 26 27 28 29     27 28                     27 28 29 30 31
30 31

         APRIL                     MAY                      JUNE
S  M  T  W  T  F  S       S  M  T  W  T  F  S       S  M  T  W  T  F  S
                  1  2    1  2  3  4  5  6  7                1  2  3  4
3  4  5  6  7  8  9       8  9 10 11 12 13 14       5  6  7  8  9 10 11
10 11 12 13 14 15 16     15 16 17 18 19 20 21      12 13 14 15 16 17 18
17 18 19 20 21 22 23     22 23 24 25 26 27 28      19 20 21 22 23 24 25
24 25 26 27 28 29 30     29 30 31                  26 27 28 29 30

         JULY                    AUGUST                  SEPTEMBER
S  M  T  W  T  F  S       S  M  T  W  T  F  S       S  M  T  W  T  F  S
               1  2       1  2  3  4  5  6                1  2  3
3  4  5  6  7  8  9       7  8  9 10 11 12 13       4  5  6  7  8  9 10
10 11 12 13 14 15 16     14 15 16 17 18 19 20      11 12 13 14 15 16 17
17 18 19 20 21 22 23     21 22 23 24 25 26 27      18 19 20 21 22 23 24
24 25 26 27 28 29 30     28 29 30 31               25 26 27 28 29 30
31

        OCTOBER                  NOVEMBER                 DECEMBER
S  M  T  W  T  F  S       S  M  T  W  T  F  S       S  M  T  W  T  F  S
                  1             1  2  3  4  5                1  2  3
2  3  4  5  6  7  8       6  7  8  9 10 11 12       4  5  6  7  8  9 10
9 10 11 12 13 14 15      13 14 15 16 17 18 19      11 12 13 14 15 16 17
16 17 18 19 20 21 22     20 21 22 23 24 25 26      18 19 20 21 22 23 24
23 24 25 26 27 28 29     27 28 29 30               25 26 27 28 29 30 31
30 31
```

J

```
        JANUARY                  FEBRUARY                  MARCH
S  M  T  W  T  F  S       S  M  T  W  T  F  S       S  M  T  W  T  F  S
1  2  3  4  5  6  7                1  2  3  4                1  2  3  4
8  9 10 11 12 13 14       5  6  7  8  9 10 11       5  6  7  8  9 10 11
15 16 17 18 19 20 21     12 13 14 15 16 17 18      12 13 14 15 16 17 18
22 23 24 25 26 27 28     19 20 21 22 23 24 25      19 20 21 22 23 24 25
29 30 31                 26 27 28                  26 27 28 29 30 31

         APRIL                     MAY                      JUNE
S  M  T  W  T  F  S       S  M  T  W  T  F  S       S  M  T  W  T  F  S
                  1          1  2  3  4  5  6                   1  2  3
2  3  4  5  6  7  8       7  8  9 10 11 12 13       4  5  6  7  8  9 10
9 10 11 12 13 14 15      14 15 16 17 18 19 20      11 12 13 14 15 16 17
16 17 18 19 20 21 22     21 22 23 24 25 26 27      18 19 20 21 22 23 24
23 24 25 26 27 28 29     28 29 30 31               25 26 27 28 29 30
30

         JULY                    AUGUST                  SEPTEMBER
S  M  T  W  T  F  S       S  M  T  W  T  F  S       S  M  T  W  T  F  S
                  1             1  2  3  4  5                   1  2
2  3  4  5  6  7  8       6  7  8  9 10 11 12       3  4  5  6  7  8  9
9 10 11 12 13 14 15      13 14 15 16 17 18 19      10 11 12 13 14 15 16
16 17 18 19 20 21 22     20 21 22 23 24 25 26      17 18 19 20 21 22 23
23 24 25 26 27 28 29     27 28 29 30 31            24 25 26 27 28 29 30
30 31

        OCTOBER                  NOVEMBER                 DECEMBER
S  M  T  W  T  F  S       S  M  T  W  T  F  S       S  M  T  W  T  F  S
1  2  3  4  5  6  7                1  2  3  4                   1  2
8  9 10 11 12 13 14       5  6  7  8  9 10 11       3  4  5  6  7  8  9
15 16 17 18 19 20 21     12 13 14 15 16 17 18      10 11 12 13 14 15 16
22 23 24 25 26 27 28     19 20 21 22 23 24 25      17 18 19 20 21 22 23
29 30 31                 26 27 28 29 30            24 25 26 27 28 29 30
                                                   31
```

K

JANUARY
```
S  M  T  W  T  F  S
      1  2  3  4  5  6
 7  8  9 10 11 12 13
14 15 16 17 18 19 20
21 22 23 24 25 26 27
28 29 30 31
```

FEBRUARY
```
S  M  T  W  T  F  S
            1  2  3
 4  5  6  7  8  9 10
11 12 13 14 15 16 17
18 19 20 21 22 23 24
25 26 27 28
```

MARCH
```
S  M  T  W  T  F  S
            1  2  3
 4  5  6  7  8  9 10
11 12 13 14 15 16 17
18 19 20 21 22 23 24
25 26 27 28 29 30 31
```

APRIL
```
S  M  T  W  T  F  S
 1  2  3  4  5  6  7
 8  9 10 11 12 13 14
15 16 17 18 19 20 21
22 23 24 25 26 27 28
29 30
```

MAY
```
S  M  T  W  T  F  S
       1  2  3  4  5
 6  7  8  9 10 11 12
13 14 15 16 17 18 19
20 21 22 23 24 25 26
27 28 29 30 31
```

JUNE
```
S  M  T  W  T  F  S
                1  2
 3  4  5  6  7  8  9
10 11 12 13 14 15 16
17 18 19 20 21 22 23
24 25 26 27 28 29 30
```

JULY
```
S  M  T  W  T  F  S
 1  2  3  4  5  6  7
 8  9 10 11 12 13 14
15 16 17 18 19 20 21
22 23 24 25 26 27 28
29 30 31
```

AUGUST
```
S  M  T  W  T  F  S
          1  2  3  4
 5  6  7  8  9 10 11
12 13 14 15 16 17 18
19 20 21 22 23 24 25
26 27 28 29 30 31
```

SEPTEMBER
```
S  M  T  W  T  F  S
                   1
 2  3  4  5  6  7  8
 9 10 11 12 13 14 15
16 17 18 19 20 21 22
23 24 25 26 27 28 29
30
```

OCTOBER
```
S  M  T  W  T  F  S
    1  2  3  4  5  6
 7  8  9 10 11 12 13
14 15 16 17 18 19 20
21 22 23 24 25 26 27
28 29 30 31
```

NOVEMBER
```
S  M  T  W  T  F  S
             1  2  3
 4  5  6  7  8  9 10
11 12 13 14 15 16 17
18 19 20 21 22 23 24
25 26 27 28 29 30
```

DECEMBER
```
S  M  T  W  T  F  S
                   1
 2  3  4  5  6  7  8
 9 10 11 12 13 14 15
16 17 18 19 20 21 22
23 24 25 26 27 28 29
30 31
```

L

JANUARY
```
S  M  T  W  T  F  S
       1  2  3  4  5
 6  7  8  9 10 11 12
13 14 15 16 17 18 19
20 21 22 23 24 25 26
27 28 29 30 31
```

FEBRUARY
```
S  M  T  W  T  F  S
                1  2
 3  4  5  6  7  8  9
10 11 12 13 14 15 16
17 18 19 20 21 22 23
24 25 26 27 28
```

MARCH
```
S  M  T  W  T  F  S
                   1
 2  3  4  5  6  7  8
 9 10 11 12 13 14 15
16 17 18 19 20 21 22
23 24 25 26 27 28 29
30 31
```

APRIL
```
S  M  T  W  T  F  S
       1  2  3  4  5
 6  7  8  9 10 11 12
13 14 15 16 17 18 19
20 21 22 23 24 25 26
27 28 29 30
```

MAY
```
S  M  T  W  T  F  S
             1  2  3
 4  5  6  7  8  9 10
11 12 13 14 15 16 17
18 19 20 21 22 23 24
25 26 27 28 29 30 31
```

JUNE
```
S  M  T  W  T  F  S
 1  2  3  4  5  6  7
 8  9 10 11 12 13 14
15 16 17 18 19 20 21
22 23 24 25 26 27 28
29 30
```

JULY
```
S  M  T  W  T  F  S
       1  2  3  4  5
 6  7  8  9 10 11 12
13 14 15 16 17 18 19
20 21 22 23 24 25 26
27 28 29 30 31
```

AUGUST
```
S  M  T  W  T  F  S
                1  2
 3  4  5  6  7  8  9
10 11 12 13 14 15 16
17 18 19 20 21 22 23
24 25 26 27 28 29 30
31
```

SEPTEMBER
```
S  M  T  W  T  F  S
    1  2  3  4  5  6
 7  8  9 10 11 12 13
14 15 16 17 18 19 20
21 22 23 24 25 26 27
28 29 30
```

OCTOBER
```
S  M  T  W  T  F  S
          1  2  3  4
 5  6  7  8  9 10 11
12 13 14 15 16 17 18
19 20 21 22 23 24 25
26 27 28 29 30 31
```

NOVEMBER
```
S  M  T  W  T  F  S
                   1
 2  3  4  5  6  7  8
 9 10 11 12 13 14 15
16 17 18 19 20 21 22
23 24 25 26 27 28 29
30
```

DECEMBER
```
S  M  T  W  T  F  S
    1  2  3  4  5  6
 7  8  9 10 11 12 13
14 15 16 17 18 19 20
21 22 23 24 25 26 27
28 29 30 31
```

M

JANUARY
```
S  M  T  W  T  F  S
             1  2  3
 4  5  6  7  8  9 10
11 12 13 14 15 16 17
18 19 20 21 22 23 24
25 26 27 28 29 30 31
```

FEBRUARY
```
S  M  T  W  T  F  S
 1  2  3  4  5  6  7
 8  9 10 11 12 13 14
15 16 17 18 19 20 21
22 23 24 25 26 27 28
```

MARCH
```
S  M  T  W  T  F  S
 1  2  3  4  5  6  7
 8  9 10 11 12 13 14
15 16 17 18 19 20 21
22 23 24 25 26 27 28
29 30 31
```

APRIL
```
S  M  T  W  T  F  S
          1  2  3  4
 5  6  7  8  9 10 11
12 13 14 15 16 17 18
19 20 21 22 23 24 25
26 27 28 29 30
```

MAY
```
S  M  T  W  T  F  S
                1  2
 3  4  5  6  7  8  9
10 11 12 13 14 15 16
17 18 19 20 21 22 23
24 25 26 27 28 29 30
31
```

JUNE
```
S  M  T  W  T  F  S
    1  2  3  4  5  6
 7  8  9 10 11 12 13
14 15 16 17 18 19 20
21 22 23 24 25 26 27
28 29 30
```

JULY
```
S  M  T  W  T  F  S
          1  2  3  4
 5  6  7  8  9 10 11
12 13 14 15 16 17 18
19 20 21 22 23 24 25
26 27 28 29 30 31
```

AUGUST
```
S  M  T  W  T  F  S
                   1
 2  3  4  5  6  7  8
 9 10 11 12 13 14 15
16 17 18 19 20 21 22
23 24 25 26 27 28 29
30 31
```

SEPTEMBER
```
S  M  T  W  T  F  S
       1  2  3  4  5
 6  7  8  9 10 11 12
13 14 15 16 17 18 19
20 21 22 23 24 25 26
27 28 29 30
```

OCTOBER
```
S  M  T  W  T  F  S
             1  2  3
 4  5  6  7  8  9 10
11 12 13 14 15 16 17
18 19 20 21 22 23 24
25 26 27 28 29 30 31
```

NOVEMBER
```
S  M  T  W  T  F  S
 1  2  3  4  5  6  7
 8  9 10 11 12 13 14
15 16 17 18 19 20 21
22 23 24 25 26 27 28
29 30
```

DECEMBER
```
S  M  T  W  T  F  S
       1  2  3  4  5
 6  7  8  9 10 11 12
13 14 15 16 17 18 19
20 21 22 23 24 25 26
27 28 29 30 31
```

N

JANUARY
```
S  M  T  W  T  F  S
                1  2
 3  4  5  6  7  8  9
10 11 12 13 14 15 16
17 18 19 20 21 22 23
24 25 26 27 28 29 30
31
```

FEBRUARY
```
S  M  T  W  T  F  S
    1  2  3  4  5  6
 7  8  9 10 11 12 13
14 15 16 17 18 19 20
21 22 23 24 25 26 27
28
```

MARCH
```
S  M  T  W  T  F  S
    1  2  3  4  5  6
 7  8  9 10 11 12 13
14 15 16 17 18 19 20
21 22 23 24 25 26 27
28 29 30 31
```

APRIL
```
S  M  T  W  T  F  S
          1  2  3
 4  5  6  7  8  9 10
11 12 13 14 15 16 17
18 19 20 21 22 23 24
25 26 27 28 29 30
```

MAY
```
S  M  T  W  T  F  S
                   1
 2  3  4  5  6  7  8
 9 10 11 12 13 14 15
16 17 18 19 20 21 22
23 24 25 26 27 28 29
30 31
```

JUNE
```
S  M  T  W  T  F  S
       1  2  3  4  5
 6  7  8  9 10 11 12
13 14 15 16 17 18 19
20 21 22 23 24 25 26
27 28 29 30
```

JULY
```
S  M  T  W  T  F  S
             1  2  3
 4  5  6  7  8  9 10
11 12 13 14 15 16 17
18 19 20 21 22 23 24
25 26 27 28 29 30 31
```

AUGUST
```
S  M  T  W  T  F  S
 1  2  3  4  5  6  7
 8  9 10 11 12 13 14
15 16 17 18 19 20 21
22 23 24 25 26 27 28
29 30 31
```

SEPTEMBER
```
S  M  T  W  T  F  S
          1  2  3  4
 5  6  7  8  9 10 11
12 13 14 15 16 17 18
19 20 21 22 23 24 25
26 27 28 29 30
```

OCTOBER
```
S  M  T  W  T  F  S
                1  2
 3  4  5  6  7  8  9
10 11 12 13 14 15 16
17 18 19 20 21 22 23
24 25 26 27 28 29 30
31
```

NOVEMBER
```
S  M  T  W  T  F  S
    1  2  3  4  5  6
 7  8  9 10 11 12 13
14 15 16 17 18 19 20
21 22 23 24 25 26 27
28 29 30
```

DECEMBER
```
S  M  T  W  T  F  S
          1  2  3  4
 5  6  7  8  9 10 11
12 13 14 15 16 17 18
19 20 21 22 23 24 25
26 27 28 29 30 31
```

VOCABULARY STUDY

Read the new words and their definitions. Then use the words correctly by writing them in the spaces that follow.

bolt — to dart off or away; flee

decoy — a person who draws another into a position where he might be trapped or robbed

determined — having a decided purpose; firm

diary — a book for keeping a daily record of experiences

immediately — without delay

interrupt — to break in upon some action or conversation

petty — small in nature or amount

Too many _____ crimes are being committed in the park. This time I am _____ to catch those thieves before they _____. I will hide in the bushes and wait for them to strike.

I need someone to attract the thieves to the scene. So you will be my _____. Just sit on the bench and pretend to be busy writing in your _____. Make sure to leave your wallet in clear view on the bench. When they reach for it, I will _____ them in the act of stealing. Then we will take them to the police station _____.

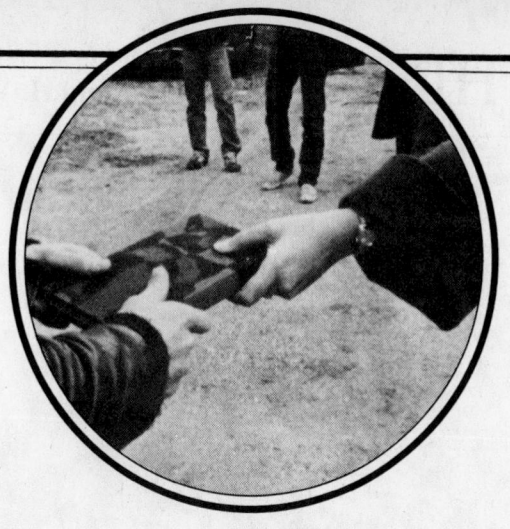

PETTY THIEF

Do you ever watch strangers and wonder who they are? Do you wonder where they are going or what they are thinking?

In this story, someone wishes to know more about a "certain stranger." He doesn't give up. But sometimes, the truth can hurt.

PETTY THIEF by Megan Stine and H. William Stine

It's hard to say exactly why Harvey first noticed the girl. Certainly, she was the most beautiful girl he had ever seen. But there were other things about her too. Maybe the fact that she was on the same crosstown bus after school for three days in a row. Maybe the fact that she bundled up in her clothes even though the weather was warm. Harvey thought she looked like she was trying to hide in them. Maybe he noticed her because she never looked very happy.

Or maybe it was the diary she was keeping. Every day, as soon as she got a seat, she took out a small writing book. She wrote the whole time until Harvey's stop.

After about a week of watching her,

Harvey was dying to read her diary. But he knew she was not going to be the easiest person in the world to meet.

For a while Harvey tried standing in front of her when she sat. But she never noticed him. Then, finally, one day there was an empty seat next to her. Harvey sat down immediately.

"Keeping a diary?" Harvey asked.

She inched away from him in her seat and twisted the book sideways so he couldn't see it.

"I used to keep one too," Harvey said. "But I stopped. Nothing exciting ever happened to me."

She closed the book. Her silence made Harvey more nervous by the minute — but more determined.

Then it was time for Harvey to get off. When he stepped off the bus, he turned to look at her again. She had gone back to writing in the diary, and she didn't look up.

Harvey couldn't get that girl out of his mind the whole night. The next day he tried finding out her name. But again she said nothing and the bus came to Harvey's stop.

Harvey got up and walked to the back of the bus. But he didn't get out of the bus at his stop. Instead, he took a seat in the back and waited to see where she got off.

A little while later, the girl got up. She walked to the back door of the bus and pushed her way to stand near the door.

"What's the matter? You in a big hurry or something?" A large woman said to her angrily.

The girl didn't answer. The bus stopped and the doors opened. But just as they opened, the girl dropped some change and bent over to pick up the money.

"Oh, for heaven's sake!" the large woman behind her said. "I thought you were in a hurry."

Take it easy, lady, Harvey thought to himself. *She dropped her money. It can happen to anyone.*

Harvey helped the people who were picking up the change. But the girl got out and started walking away before Harvey could catch up with her.

"Hey, wait," Harvey called. He had to walk fast to catch up with her. "Here's a quarter you dropped," Harvey said.

She took the quarter out of Harvey's hand and kept walking without saying anything. But she looked more unhappy than ever.

Then Harvey noticed for the first time that they were in an alley behind some stores and restaurants. A group of kids were sitting on the back steps. One of the guys, a really big guy, got up and came toward Harvey and the girl. The guy put his arm around the girl and gave her a quick kiss. Harvey didn't like him from the start.

"What do you want?" the guy said in a low, tough voice.

"Nothing," Harvey said.

"Marie's *my* girl," the guy said.

Harvey was glad to know the girl's name.

"*Your* girl," Harvey said. "You sound like you own her."

The guy started coming for Harvey. He was about three inches taller and 30 pounds heavier than Harvey. Harvey tried to back up slowly but the

guy kept moving closer.

Quickly, Harvey started kicking over the metal garbage cans that were lined up behind the buildings. Crash after crash until finally one of the back doors opened.

"Hey! What the devil is going on back there?" A bald man poked his head out the door. "You kids get out of here before I call the cops! You hear me?"

Marie pulled on her boyfriend's arm and the whole gang ran down the alley. Marie looked back at Harvey once.

Harvey walked back to the bus stop thinking of her name and remembering the way she looked back at him.

The next day, Harvey missed his usual bus and caught a later one. He was surprised to see that Marie was also on the late bus. Another girl Har-vey had seen with the gang got on too. But she and Marie acted like they didn't know each other.

"Hi," Harvey said.

Marie looked up at him. "Leave me alone, will you?" she said.

Harvey could tell she really meant it, but he just couldn't do it.

"Are you really going with that guy?" Harvey asked.

She didn't answer.

"Are you?" Harvey asked again.

"No," she said angrily.

"Good," Harvey said. "Then why can't..."

"I have to go," she interrupted him and got up.

Just like the day before, she pushed her way to stand on the steps at the back of the bus. Harvey thought she was just trying to get away from him in a hurry. But when the bus stopped, Marie dropped her purse again. And her money fell out all over the steps.

Then Harvey saw what was really happening. While the people were helping Marie pick up her change, Marie's friend was stealing a woman's wallet.

Harvey looked around. No one saw the thief. Everyone on the bus was watching Marie.

"Wait! Stop!" Harvey called out.

As soon as he shouted, Marie left the bus. Marie's friend dropped the wallet and took off. Harvey bolted out the door, but the crowd slowed him down.

"That girl just tried to steal your wallet," Harvey told the woman. "You'd better be more careful."

"Thanks, I will," the woman said, picking up her wallet from the sidewalk.

Marie was gone, of course, but Harvey figured he knew where she was heading. He ran to catch up. He was angry, but he felt sick too.

"That girl is your friend. You know she's a thief. And you're her decoy, aren't you?" Harvey shouted at her.

"Get lost," Marie shouted back.

"Why do you do it? What do you have to do that for?" Harvey was still shouting as they walked.

But when Harvey looked away from her, he saw the gang coming toward them. The big guy was leading them, and Marie's friend was there too.

"I want to see you again," Harvey said.

"You can't," Marie told him. Then she reached into her purse and took out her diary. She handed it to Harvey and then ran to meet her friends. Harvey didn't stay to find out what happened. He turned and walked home with her diary in his hand.

The diary was the saddest book Harvey ever read.

———————————

READING CHECK

WORD MEANING FROM CONTEXT

1. "She bundled up in her clothes" probably means that _____ .
   a. she tied up her clothes in a neat package
   b. she snuggled deep into her clothes
   c. she cried all over her dress

MAIN IDEA

2. This story is about a girl who _____

_____ .

DETAILS

3. Harvey noticed that each day the girl would _____

_____ until the bus came to her stop.

4. Harvey saw that the girl never looked _____ .

SEQUENCE

5. When Marie dropped her purse, her friend would _____

_____ .

FINDING PROOF

6. Harvey cared about Marie. Proof is that _____ _____ .

CAUSE AND EFFECT

7. Marie and the other girl on the bus acted as if they didn't know each other because _____ .

WHAT DO YOU THINK?

Do you think Marie had any feelings for Harvey? Why do you think she gave him her diary? What do you think her life was like? After reading Marie's diary, do you think Harvey would still want to see her again? What answer might the diary give to Harvey's question: "What do you have to do that for?"

Can you think of any way that Harvey might help Marie? Do you think Marie wants help?

WORDS IN CONTEXT

The 10 words below in boldface are from the story you've just read. They also belong in the joke. But they are in mixed-up order. Read the joke. Then, in the spaces that follow, write the words in their correct order. The first one is done for you.

Julie Farber, an off-duty **usual,** said good night to her **alley** and headed home. She got off the **nervous** bus and took her **sake** shortcut through the **twist**. Suddenly, she heard loud cries for help. A big **crosstown** man was trying to **angrily** the arm of a much smaller man.

"Hey, you!" Julie shouted **boyfriend**. "Leave him alone, for heaven's **cop!**" Julie was a little **tough**, but she jumped into the fight anyway. When she pushed the big guy aside, he ran off.

"Thanks," said the little guy after he pulled himself together. "That was real nice of you. I'll tell you what—we can share the twenty bucks I took from him."

1. _____*Cop*_____   6. _____

2. _____   7. _____

3. _____   8. _____

4. _____   9. _____

5. _____   10. _____

MAIN IDEA

Suppose someone is telling you a joke. The joke goes on and on without anything funny happening. Finally you say, "Get to the point!" What you want is the main idea—the part that makes the story a joke.

A good punch line sums up the main idea of a joke. Reread the joke on page 102. Then look at the three sentences below. Check the one that sums up the main point of the story.

_____ 1. **Julie took a shortcut through the alley.**

_____ 2. **The little guy Julie helped turned out to be the thief.**

_____ 3. **The big man ran off.**

Sentences 1 and 3 give details or small parts of the story. But sentence 2 tells about the story as a whole. Sentence 2, then, sums up the main idea of the joke.

The main idea of a joke or story is its most important point. Sometimes main ideas are hard to pin down. One way to spot them is to make up newspaper headlines for the stories or articles you read.

A good headline tells in a few words what an article is about. It can't be too general. But it can't be too specific in detail either.

Look at the three headlines below. Check the one that would make the best headline for the joke. Which headline is too general or broad? Which one has to do with a detail instead of the whole story?

_____ **Street Crimes**

_____ **Two Men Come to Blows in Street**

_____ **Off-Duty Cop Helps Wrong Man**

VOCABULARY STUDY

downpour   involve   license   splatter
fender   joyride   menu   spree

Write the words in the puzzle below. When you are done, you will have the complete answer to this riddle:

Riddle: **When is a car not a car?**
Answer: *When it's turning into a* _____ .

a. protection for a car   _ _ _ ☐ _ _

b. unchecked outburst of activity;
going on a shopping ___   _ _ ☐ _ _

c. card that gives permission to
drive   _ ☐ _ _ _ _ _

d. to include; draw in   _ _ ☐ _ _ _ _

e. a list of dishes that are served   _ ☐ _ _

f. a heavy rainfall   _ _ ☐ _ _ _ _ _

g. spill; splash; make dirty   _ _ _ ☐ _ _ _

h. a pleasure ride that is
marked by careless driving   _ _ ☐ _ _ _ _

THE JOYRIDE

What if a stranger offered to let you try out his car? Some people would jump at the chance. Jim did. But will he bring it back? His friend wonders. . . .

THE JOYRIDE — by C. Turner

One day last summer, a Lincoln Continental pulled up in front of my father's restaurant. It was the middle of the afternoon. My father had gone to the bank. Jim was filling the saltshakers. I was changing the menus. You don't see a Lincoln Continental in this town very often. And I noticed that Jim spilled some salt when he looked out the window.

The driver came in and sat at the counter. He ordered coffee.

"That's a real machine you have out there," Jim said.

"It sure is," the man said.

Jim went outside for a closer look. I went back to the menus. But I watched Jim, and so did the man.

Jim walked a slow circle around the car. I don't think his eyes missed an inch. He stood for a long time facing the hood. Finally he reached out and ran his fingers over the gleaming surface. Then he put his hands in his pockets.

"I can remember my first car," the man said. "It was a long time ago, but I can remember it very well. How old is he?"

"Sixteen," I said.

Jim's eyes were still large when he came in.

"Do you drive?" the man asked him.

"Sure."

"Do you have a license?"

"Sure."

I thought I knew what was coming, but I couldn't believe it.

"How would you like to take her down the road a mile or two?" the man said.

Jim stared at him. "Are you serious?" he asked.

"Yes." The man was holding out the keys.

Jim shot a glance at me. He seemed to be saying, *Should I?*

I didn't know what to say. And he didn't wait for an answer. He took the keys and hurried outside.

I was thinking about something I didn't want to think about. Jim had spent some time in a "home" up in Frankfield, for stealing a car for a two-day driving spree. Everybody around here knew about it and still talked about what a shame it was.

Nobody thought Jim was worth much. I'd had to do a lot of talking to get my father to hire him. I told my father I was sure Jim had changed. I kept saying Jim would never be able to prove it unless someone gave him a chance.

I still felt that I was right. But I admit I didn't feel easy as I watched Jim drive off in the Lincoln Continental. Somehow it seemed that I was almost as involved as he was.

When I finished changing the menus, I wiped the counter from one end to the other. I poured some more coffee for the man and tried to think of something to say.

I talked about the downpour we'd had that morning. The man said he'd had good weather so far. I asked him where he was heading. He said California.

He started telling me about California. I thought I was listening. But suddenly I realized I wasn't tuned in at all. I looked at my watch. Fifteen minutes had passed since Jim had driven off. Fifteen minutes was too long, the way I figured it.

Sixteen minutes.

Seventeen minutes.

Eighteen minutes.

I was getting worried.

When the man went to the rest room, I went outside and looked down the road. There was no car in sight.

"Jim, you're crazy," I whispered.

I went inside. The man was coming out of the rest room.

"More coffee?" I asked.

He said he'd had plenty. He paid his check and stood at the window and waited.

I kept looking at my watch. Jim had been gone almost half an hour.

The man said, "You don't suppose he has had an accident, do you?"

"No, I think he's having a whirl," I answered.

The man turned and looked at me. I couldn't look him in the eye. I just stared out the window.

The next instant, I was smiling. I could see the Lincoln Continental coming down the road, sharp in the sun.

"Here he comes," I said.

Jim told us about the mud. It had splattered on the fenders when he pulled off the road to turn around. He had driven to the service station to give the car a quick wash.

"I couldn't bring this machine back with mud on her," he said.

Jim and I watched the man drive off.

"Did you tell him about me?" Jim asked.

"No," I said.

"I want the truth. Did you tell him about me?"

"I'm telling the truth."

"I'll bet you were surprised when I — "

I didn't want him to say it, so I interrupted him. "Sure, I was surprised. I never heard of a guy offering his Lincoln Continental to a stranger for a joyride. I never heard of anything like that in all my life."

READING CHECK

WORD MEANING FROM CONTEXT

1. In the story, the word *Lincoln* means ____ .
   a. the name of a U.S. president
   b. a town in Nebraska
   c. a kind of car

MAIN IDEA

2. Another title for this story could be ____ .
   a. First Car
   b. A Second Chance
   c. The Stranger

DETAILS

3. Jim had spent time in a "home" for _____ .

SEQUENCE

4. Number these events in the order in which they happened.

____ Jim stopped at a service station.

____ Jim admired the Lincoln Continental.

____ The stranger gave Jim the keys to the car.

____ Jim spent time in a "home."

____ Jim got the job in the restaurant.

____ Jim drove off in the Lincoln Continental.

FINDING PROOF

5. Jim wondered if his friend had trusted him. Proof is that _____

_____ .

CAUSE AND EFFECT

6. Draw a line from each cause to its effect.

Causes	Effects
Jim admired the Lincoln Continental.	The narrator kept checking her watch.
Jim stole a car.	Jim got the car washed.
Jim had been gone a long time.	Jim spent time in a "home."
The car got splattered with mud.	The stranger let Jim drive the car.

WHAT DO YOU THINK?

Why did the narrator persuade her father to hire Jim? How does the narrator feel as Jim first drives off in the Lincoln Continental? How does the narrator feel when Jim has not returned after almost half an hour? Why is Jim so late in returning? Do you believe what he says about the mud?

FINDING PROOF

The detective thinks the chauffeur killed Mr. Biggs. How does she know? How can she prove that his story is a lie? Look at the last picture. Do you notice anything that disproves the chauffeur's story? (Hint: The chauffeur said the car was in rain and mud.)

In mysteries, detectives look at all the evidence. Then they come to a conclusion. But they need proof to solve the case and back up what they think.

All stories are like mysteries until you read and understand them. When you read, you draw conclusions about the characters. You figure out the story's message or what it is about. But just like a detective, you have to find proof for the conclusions you come to.

Think, for example, of the story "The Joyride." You could say that the narrator believed in giving people a second chance. How do you know that to be true? Proof is that she persuaded her father to hire Jim. Can you find other proof in the story? Write it below.

Proof is that _____

_____ .

To know if a conclusion is correct, there must be proof to back it up. But remember: the proof must be in the story.

Read the boldface parts from the story, and **draw a conclusion** by completing each sentence that follows. Then go back to the story and **find proof** that your answer is correct.

1. **"That's a real machine you have out there," Jim said.**
   Jim said this because _____ .
   a. he wanted to buy the car
   b. he was crazy about cars
   c. he was about to steal the car

Proof is that _____

_____ .

2. **"How would you like to take her down the road a mile or two?"**
the man said.
The man wanted Jim to drive his car because _____ .
a. the man thought Jim was someone else
b. the man was tired and wanted Jim to take over for a while
c. the man remembered what it was like to be young and want to
drive a big car

Proof is that _____

_____ .

3. **"Sure I was surprised. I never heard of a guy offering his Lin-**
coln Continental to a stranger for a joyride."
The narrator interrupted Jim because _____ .
a. she was rude
b. Jim was dragging out a story
c. she didn't want Jim to think she hadn't trusted him

Proof is that _____

_____ .

What do you think? Do you think the narrator was a good friend? Yes
or No? Find proof in the story to support your opinion.

I think the narrator _____ (**was, was not**) a good friend.

The reason I feel this way is that she _____

_____ .

VOCABULARY STUDY

chuckle   especially   mumbled   stereo
confused   motorcycle   pretend

Write these words in the story below. When you are done, you will have a complete joke.

Bill was riding his _____ when he met his friends Gus and Sue. "I'm _____ glad to see you two," he said. "Come over to my house. We can listen to my new _____."

Bill lived on the 20th floor of a tall building. When they got there, they found that the elevator was out of order.

Gus looked _____. "What do we do now?"

"Let's _____ we're mountain climbers," Bill suggested. "The climb won't seem so hard if we pass the time away. One of you should sing a song for us. The other should tell a joke and make us _____. Then I will tell a sad, sad story."

When they reached the 19th floor, it was Bill's turn to tell his sad story. He did. "I left the key downstairs," he _____.

A PLACE
TO
CALL HOME

If someone took away the thing you loved most, what would you do? Bess believed in fighting for her rights. But then, her enemy surprised her.

A PLACE TO CALL HOME

by Phillis Fair Cowell

I don't like waiting, especially for something I don't want. But that was all I could do. It was happening, whether I liked it or not. So I looked out the window and watched the rain. Behind me, my mother folded laundry. I should have been helping. Instead, I asked the question one more time.

"Why does he have to come live with us?" I mumbled out the window.

My mother sighed. "You're not a four-year-old, you know. You don't have to ask that over and over." She sighed again. "He's old. He can't take care of himself anymore."

I turned toward her and blurted out the words. "There are homes for people like that!"

She stared at me for several seconds. Her voice was low when she spoke. "Don't say that again, Bess," she said.

I turned back to the window, the rain, and my thoughts. It wasn't that I hated my grandfather. I didn't remember him enough to hate him. When I was little, I spent summers on his farm. But that was a long time ago. All I remembered was the smell of the pigs and the look of the pictures. They were old-fashioned pictures, and they seemed to cover every wall. When my grandmother died, I stopped going down there. Only my dad went, once a year, to visit his father.

I really didn't care if my grandfather lived in this house. He could live anywhere — except my room.

That room meant a lot to me. It was my private place. Most of the money from my job went into that room. I bought the red curtains and rug and furry pillows. I painted it bright yellow and put wild posters on the walls. It was me, from top to bottom.

Now I was being tucked into a pink and white corner, my little sister's room. I had a right to be angry.

Anger didn't keep it from happening. The car pulled up. My father jumped out and rushed to the other side. I watched as he helped the old man out of the car.

My grandfather seemed smaller than I remembered. And he moved much more slowly. But it wasn't slow enough for me.

At the door, there were hugs and kisses. I pretended to be glad to see him.

He sat and talked a while. Then he said he was tired and he went to lie down in his room. *My room!*

That really bothered me. I stormed into the living room and turned on the stereo. I started playing one of my

119

records loudly. My mother came in and turned it off.

"Sh," she said. "He's trying to take a nap."

I exploded. "Don't *I* belong anywhere in this house?" I yelled. Then I ran to my sister's room. I was glad she wasn't home. At least I could cry in private.

Between sobs, I thought a lot. I couldn't understand it. No one cared what I was going through. All they cared about was that old man. He had it made now — food service, laundry service, maid service. He must think this is heaven.

Suddenly, I thought of my radio. I had a right to have it. But it, and a lot of my things, were still in my old room. If I tried to get my radio, I might wake him.

I didn't care. If he woke up, I'd tell him how I felt. I'd tell him what he'd done to me. Maybe he didn't know. If he knew, maybe he'd leave. I had to have it out with him sooner or later.

I opened his door quietly. What I saw almost made me laugh. He looked so out of place in my brightly colored room. He lay, face down, under his old gray blanket. It made him seem older and grayer somehow. Above his head hung my motorcycle poster. The cycle looked as if it were about to roar right over him.

"It hurts, doesn't it?" he said,

without moving.

His voice surprised me. "What?" I said.

"Giving up your own place," he said.

I didn't know what to say. I sure couldn't argue with that. They were the only words that had made sense all day.

"They say you get used to it," he said. "I don't know. I had my place for more than forty years."

"How did you know this was my room?" I asked.

He laughed and turned over to face me. "It looks like you," he said. "I remember how you were — bright and bold." He chuckled. Then his face became sad. "*My* place looked like me."

I was getting upset. Our talk wasn't supposed to be like this. I was supposed to attack. I was supposed to fight for my rights. But he understood. He knew how I felt.

I hurried across the room and picked up my radio. "I just came in for this," I said.

As I closed the door, I heard him mumble. "I had that house for more than forty years. I don't even know the folks who own it now."

I stood outside the door, feeling confused. Today was filled with loss. I had lost my room, and I had lost my fight.

Tomorrow. Maybe tomorrow I would give the old man a hard time and make him want to leave. Of course, he had lost something too. Maybe, instead, I would buy some old-fashioned pictures for his room.

READING CHECK

WORD MEANING FROM CONTEXT

1. In this story, the word *exploded* means _____ .
   a. something blew up into bits
   b. someone got angry and spoke out
   c. an idea was proved to be wrong

MAIN IDEA

2. This story is about _____

_____ .

DETAILS

3. Some things in Bess's room seemed wrong for her grandfather. They

were _____

_____ .

4. Bess wondered if she should buy some _____

for her grandfather.

SEQUENCE

5. Bess spent summers at her grandfather's farm when _____

_____ .

FINDING PROOF

6. The old man understood Bess's feelings. Proof is that _____

_____.

CAUSE AND EFFECT

7. The old man had come to live with his family because _____

_____.

WHAT DO YOU THINK?

What problems might the grandfather have in getting used to his new home? Do you think Bess will give him a hard time? Or will she buy him some new pictures? If you were Bess, what would you do? Why? In what ways are Bess and her grandfather different? How are they alike? Do you think they have much in common?

READING
DESCRIPTIONS

Do you understand descriptions? Can you picture or feel what is being described?

Descriptions are important in reading. You can't understand what you read unless you know what the people, places, things, and feelings are like. The author usually tells you about these, to help you enjoy the story.

Read each of the following paragraphs. Then look at the drawings. Add to, or change each drawing so it fits the description. Be sure to read carefully, so you don't miss any part of the description.

It was hard not to stare at the man who was walking down Main Street. He wore an old-fashioned bathing suit with wide stripes. On his head was a high pointed hat. He carried an umbrella with "Buy Savings Bonds" on it. In his other hand, he held a pitchfork with a bow tied on the handle. He had on leather boots and wore heart-shaped eyeglasses.

Eleanor saw some objects on the table. There was half an orange, with a small flag stuck into it. A dog's face had been painted on a large, flat rock. Next to the rock was a small skull, made out of glass. A set of false teeth could be seen beside it. Next to the teeth was a birthday cake with seven candles.

The castle stood on a high cliff, looking down on the sea. It had three towers, with long windows in each of them. Sheep were grazing on the grass in front of the castle. A cage stood under a tall tree. In the cage was a fat lion, sound asleep. On top of the cage was a bird. The bird was spreading its wings and singing.

Now you try. In "A Place to Call Home," Bess's grandfather says that her room looks like her — bright and bold. Draw a picture of Bess's room as she describes it in the story. Then, add the things you think will make the room suit her grandfather. Bess gives you one idea at the end of the story. What others can you think of?

WHAT'S YOUR OPINION?

Mr. Martin has a good job as a welder. Mrs. Martin is a writer who works at home. They have three children. The children are Johnny, 16; Kim, 14; and Jennifer, 10.

Mrs. Martin is very worried about her 83-year-old mother. Her mother lives alone in an apartment near the Martins. She can't see very well. She has fallen down several times recently. And her mind is not as sharp as it used to be.

Mrs. Martin's mother sometimes says embarrassing things. Sometimes she gets the children's names mixed up. Once she thought Mr. Martin was someone else.

The doctor says she can no longer manage on her own. She must live with the Martins. Or she must go to a nursing home.

The Martins have different opinions about what should be done. So do Mrs. Martin's sister and brother-in-law, the Browns.

Read the following opinions. At the end, write what *you* think should be done. Or try to settle the situation with other students. Play the parts of the following seven people. You may add Mrs. Martin's mother, if you wish.

1. **Mrs. Martin:** My mother has worked hard to be a good mother and grandmother. What should she get for all that hard work? To be forgotten in an old people's home? No. She should move in with us.

2. **Mr. Martin:** I want to do the best things for my wife's mother. But I have to think of my family too. My wife doesn't have time to do her work, take care of us and her mother too. A good nursing home is the best place for my wife's mother. There she will get good care. Nurses and doctors will look after her health.

3. **Jennifer:** I love Grandma. I don't want to see her in a nursing home. My friend's grandma went to one of those places. They didn't take good care of her. She got sick. People forgot to visit her. Pretty soon she died.

4. **Johnny:** I love Grandma. But she's only one person. And she would change the lives of all five of us if she lived here. It would be hard to have friends over with Grandma here. She says funny things. She insults people. She doesn't really know what's going on. A nursing home is best.

5. **Mrs. Brown:** The situation is a very sad one. Modern medicine is to blame. People are living longer than they should. In the old days, people died before they became a burden to the rest of the family.

6. **Mr. Brown:** I don't agree with my wife. I believe in the way many Chinese families live. The whole family stays together. The old take care of the young. Then the young grow up and take care of the old.

7. **Kim:** I love Grandma. But if she lived with us, I'd have to share a room with Jennifer. I know that sounds selfish. But having my own room means so much to me. Grandma loves us and would want us to be happy. She wouldn't want to cause trouble by coming here.

8. **Your Opinion:** _____

_____

_____

_____

_____

_____

VOCABULARY STUDY

argument	holler	imagine	rifle
doubt	homestead	prairie	vacant

Words that have almost the same meanings are called *synonyms*. For example, *big* and *large* are synonyms. So are *small* and *tiny*.

Words from the story and their synonyms are hiding in the puzzle below. Begin at START. Draw a line from the word *argument* to its synonym. Move one square at a time. Find another word from the story, then go on to its synonym, and so on. Keep going until you reach the END (or *finish*!).

START

argument	strange	cook	gun	prairie	quiet
fight	dangerous	bother	rifle	grasslands	empty
doubt	question	terrible	think	vacant	homestead
helper	holler	yell	imagine	laugh	house

END

The words that are left over are synonyms for words you've already learned. Can you think of them?

THE LOT

Have you ever gotten into trouble because of boasts you have made? Why do some people "talk big"?

In this story "big talk" leads to "big trouble." As you read the story, think: Why did the author write this? Did he have something important to say? How would you have handled the situation?

THE LOT   by Ray Anthony Shepard

It was just a plain vacant lot, over near the school. When I was there by myself, I tried to imagine what it was like a long time ago, before Nebraska was a state. Sometimes, after I had seen a movie about the West, I could believe that covered wagons had passed through. And when the city

his gun, looking for animals.

Every night, Billy, Junior, and the rest of us went there to laugh and talk. There was nothing else to do.

Junior hadn't always lived in our town. He was really from Mississippi. But for some reason, he went to live with his grandmother in Chicago. It hadn't worked out, so he came here to live with a cousin or something.

When he first got here, he didn't say he was from Mississippi, even though he talked like he was. He said he was from Chicago. This was OK with us. Most of us were just from around here. It was good to know someone from Chicago, even if he had only lived there for two months. But being from Chicago meant to Junior that he was the "baddest." And I guess it meant that to the rest of us. I didn't mind so much, since I was the smallest. But Billy had other ideas.

The first time Billy and Junior tested each other, Junior won. There was no doubt about it. They didn't really fight. They just hollered at each other. Junior won because Billy had never been called so many names and not done anything about it. I guess it was because Billy had never been to a real city, even for a week.

Looking back now, that's what got Junior into trouble. His mouth could do more than his fist. He would talk

didn't cut the weeds for a time, it did look like the prairie. Maybe someone had had a homestead nearby. Maybe he used to stand where I stood, with

his way into trouble, then talk his way out. But after a while, it got harder to get out. Everybody began to think Junior was only a lot of mouth. Even I began to think I could beat him if I had to. After all, he was really from Mississippi.

One day, Junior couldn't talk fast enough, and Billy hit him in the face. Every time Junior tried to talk back, Billy would hit him again. When he finally tried to fight back, Billy did him in.

After that, I guess Junior knew he couldn't just talk. So he got himself a gun. It was a .22 pistol, which isn't much of a gun. But we had never even thought about one. We had rifles for hunting — but a pistol! Maybe two months in Chicago did make a difference.

Every time Junior's mouth got him into something his fist couldn't get him out of, out would come that gun. Even though it was small, the moonlight made it big enough to end anything Junior started. But after a while, even that wasn't enough to stop the guys from thinking Junior was just fat-mouthing again. We began to think he didn't have any bullets. Or that his gun didn't work.

I guess Billy decided to find out if it was for real. One night, he let it be known that he also had a gun. That's how it started that night. Billy hid his gun in the tall grass by the tree. Junior had his in his pocket. When the argument started, Junior brought out his gun, and Billy ran for his.

I don't think Junior really wanted to pull the trigger. But what else could he do? He just closed his eyes and pulled. When he opened his eyes and found he had missed, he had to pull the trigger again. And when that shot missed, too, Junior must have felt dumb. It looked like even his gun was going to let him down. So he pulled again and again. Billy fell to the ground, holding his leg. There was nothing for him to do, either, except fire back.

I guess the difference was that Billy had to do something to stay alive. And Junior was just trying to prove he was from Chicago, rather than Mississippi or Nebraska. Of course, staying alive is more important than where you're from. Because it was Junior who died that night in the vacant lot, over near the school. The same lot where I could believe a homesteader had once looked for something to shoot a long time ago.

READING CHECK

WORD MEANING FROM CONTEXT

1. In this story, a *vacant lot* means _____ .
   a. a way of life
   b. an empty piece of land
   c. a great amount

2. ''Junior was only a lot of mouth.'' This means that he _____ .
   a. wore braces
   b. asked a lot of questions
   c. was all talk and no action

MAIN IDEA

3. This story is about _____

   _____ .

DETAILS

4. Junior was born in _____ .

5. Junior said he was from _____ .

SEQUENCE

6. Junior got himself a gun after _____

   _____ .

7. Billy got himself a gun when _____

_____ .

FINDING PROOF

8. Junior's mouth could do more than his fist. Proof is that _____

_____ .

CAUSE AND EFFECT

9. Junior thought he had to be the "baddest" because _____

_____ .

10. Billy wanted to save his own life, so he _____ .

WHAT DO YOU THINK?

What kind of boy do you think Junior is? How do you think he feels toward the other boys? What kind of boy is Billy? What part does he play in the group of boys? How does he feel toward the new kid? Why does Junior get a gun? What do you think the others think of him then? What would you have done if you were Billy? Could the death have been avoided? How? "Staying alive is more important than where you're from." What do you think the author meant by this?

NOTING
AUTHOR'S PURPOSE

In reading, it is important to understand the author's purpose. Writers have different reasons for writing what they write. Authors of ads, for example, try to sell things. Selling is their purpose. Other writers may want to "sell" you ideas. Still others may just want to entertain or inform.

Read the groups of words below. Each one gives a reason or purpose for writing the paragraphs that follow. Next to each phrase, write the number of the paragraph that best fits the purpose.

_____ to entertain   _____ to give an opinion

_____ to inform   _____ to give directions

1. If you don't like taking pills when you're sick, this invention could help you. It's a way of taking medicine by sticking it behind your ear! The medicine comes in a small, round container that looks something like a pill. The container has special glue on one side that helps it stick to the skin. Scientists say that the skin behind the ear is soft and thin. Medicine in these containers could go through the skin little by little as the body needs it.

2. To make popcorn, use a large pot. First, cover the bottom with oil. Then add the corn. Make sure there is only one layer of corn. Cover the pot and heat until all the corn pops. Pour the popped corn into a big bowl. Sprinkle with salt and melted butter.

3. The teacher gave back the test papers. Matt looked at his mark and gasped. When the bell rang, he went to the teacher's desk.

    "I know I've been doing badly," he said. "But I don't think I deserved a zero."

    "You're right," the teacher said. "But that's the lowest mark I can give you."

4. The movie was about a little girl who gets picked up by a tornado. She lands in this silly place called OZ. Everybody sings stupid songs throughout the movie. The acting was terrible, except for the little dog named Toto. The witch was good too. All in all, it was a terrible movie.

Here are some things you were told in the story "The Lot." Choose the author's purpose for writing each.

1. **The author said the lot looked like an old prairie.** His purpose was _____.
   a. to let you know that he liked Western movies
   b. to show how some things change and how they stay the same
   c. to tell you that everything reminded him of a prairie

2. **The author told about the places Junior had lived.** His purpose was _____.
   a. to show that Junior had not had it easy
   b. to describe different parts of the country
   c. to let you know he thought it was interesting

3. **The author wrote that Billy got a gun.** His purpose was _____.
   a. to give directions
   b. to show that Billy was from Chicago
   c. to set a scene where Junior would have to prove he was the "baddest"

Whenever you read, you should ask yourself: *Why is the author telling me this?* Sometimes, you may decide that an author has more than one reason or purpose for writing.

Why do you think the author wrote the story "The Lot"? What was he saying? Here is a list of purposes. Check the ones that have to do with "The Lot."

_____ to give information

_____ to entertain

_____ to scare the reader

_____ to show that boasting can lead to trouble

_____ to show that guns are dangerous

_____ to give directions

_____ to show what can happen when there is nothing to do

_____ to give an opinion

_____ to tell why an event happened

_____ to describe ways to avoid accidents

_____ to teach a lesson

Suppose that you were the person Junior showed his gun to for the first time. You know a gun means trouble. What could you do, or say, that might save somebody's life?

Choose one of the statements below. Explain why you think it's the best idea. Or, if you have a better idea, tell why you think it would work.

1. Call the police and tell them Junior has a gun.

2. Go to the people Junior lives with and ask them to take the gun away from him.

3. Become a special friend of Junior's and try to keep him away from the lot and from Billy.

4. Tell Junior that he doesn't have to prove anything. Tell him that everybody is jealous of him, and nobody likes Billy anyway.

5. Talk to Billy and try to get him to leave Junior alone no matter what Junior says.

6. Get all the kids to gang up on Junior and take the gun away from him.

7. Get all the kids to stop speaking to Junior until he gets rid of the gun.

8. Try to get Junior to see how dumb it is to carry a gun and how he may be sorry.

_____

_____

_____

_____

_____

_____

VOCABULARY STUDY

baggy	costume	squirt	striped
cafeteria	Halloween	statue	stunt
cigar	solid	stomp	

Boss: I need someone I can count on.
Applicant: I'm very _____. Whenever something went
wrong on my old job, I was always _____.

Someone has answered a want ad. Write the new words in the puzzle below to find out what is said. Then see if you think the person should get the job.

a. something one can smoke   _ _ _ _ ☐

b. kind of restaurant   _ _ _ ☐ _ _ _ _ _

c. carved form of someone   ☐ _ _ _ _ _

d. having lines of different colors   _ _ _ _ ☐ _ _

e. to stamp with one's feet   _ _ ☐ _ _

f. something that attracts attention   _ _ _ ☐ _

g. to force out liquid;
   rhymes with *dirt*   ☐ _ _ _ _ _

h. firm; not hollow   _ _ _ ☐ _

i. loose-fitting   ☐ _ _ _ _

j. holiday in October   _ _ _ ☐ _ _ _ _ _

k. kind of dress worn
   in a show   _ _ _ _ _ _ ☐

$40
A WEEK

Luis needed money. To get it, he had to make a fool of himself. Of course, he learned that it pays to make people laugh. But his boss had to be taught another lesson.

$40 A WEEK by Megan Stine and H. William Stine

"OK, kid, you want a job?" Mr. Grogan asked.

"I sure do," said Luis.

"And you'll do anything?" Mr. Grogan chewed on an old, dead cigar as he talked.

"Yeah, sure. I'll pump gas, change tires, sweep, wash floors — anything," Luis said.

"No, kid. I've got enough guys at the gas pumps. What I need are some more customers. So I've got something in mind. I want you to put on a clown costume."

"A what?" Luis said.

"You know, a clown costume. And I want you to paint your face white and wear this big red nose while you're at it. Then you stand in the middle of the street and wave cars into the gas station. It's as simple as that."

But it wasn't that simple. Luis never had a lot of money, but he dressed sharp. He liked the way he looked. He kept mostly to himself and he never let anyone laugh at him — not to his face. So how could he let people see him in that clown suit?

"I'll pay you forty dollars a week to start," Mr. Grogan said.

Was this the job he had spent three solid weeks looking for?

"Think about it tonight. You can start tomorrow if you want. It'll be a lot of fun," Mr. Grogan said without a smile.

The next day, Luis stood in front of the mirror. He had put on a baggy, red and white striped suit. His face was all white with a big red nose. His mouth was a fat red lipstick smear and his eyebrows were big and blue. He put on a wig that looked like a red mop and a tall black hat.

"I look like a fool," Luis said. He hated to look at himself. "Everyone will laugh at me." Mr. Grogan pounded on the door. "OK, kid, let's go. Time's wasting."

Luis slowly opened the door. Mr. Grogan and his two helpers took one look and burst out laughing. Luis' fists tightened.

"OK, kid, remember our deal. If you don't get fifty new customers a week, you're fired. Now get out there," Mr. Grogan said.

Luis slowly walked into the middle of the street. He watched the cars pass him on both sides for a while.

"Talk. I'm not paying you to stand like a statue. Talk!" Mr. Grogan shouted.

But nothing came out when Luis opened his mouth. He hoped none of his friends drove by. "I've got to get six hundred dollars by summer," Luis kept reminding himself.

A car full of guys from the high school came down the street. They stopped to look at Luis.

"Drive on in to Grogan's Gas Station," Luis said softly and pointed toward the station.

"You're a little early for Halloween, aren't you?" the driver said with a snort.

Luis didn't say the first thing he thought of because he saw Mr. Grogan watching him. So Luis told the driver again to drive on in.

"Didn't you hear what I said about Halloween?" the driver said. "What are you supposed to look like?"

Luis looked him straight in the eyes and said, "Your mother."

The driver's face froze. There was going to be a fight for sure. But just then the other guys in the car started laughing.

"You know, Jack," one of the guys said to the driver, "he does look a little like your mom." And he laughed some more.

"Especially early on Saturday mornings," another said.

Then even the driver had to laugh.

"You're pretty funny for a clown," the driver said to Luis.

"You're laughing now, but wait till you see our prices," Luis said.

The driver laughed again and spun the car into the gas station.

Well, if it worked once, it could work again. So Luis started yelling different things at the passing cars.

"Drive that car in before you have to push it in!"

"You've got enough dirt on that car

to plant a garden. Drive in to Grogan's for a car wash!''

"Grogan's gives you better gas than the high school cafeteria!''

A couple of times, Luis even lay down in the middle of the street until cars stopped. And when people came rushing up to see what was the matter, Luis sat up and said, "Buy your gas at Grogan's."

A few people didn't like the stunt, but a lot of people did. Pretty soon parents were driving by with their kids to see the funny clown. Luis gave them balloons. And girls drove by to talk with the clown. They gave Luis their telephone numbers.

By the end of the week, Mr. Grogan's business was booming. Everyone was buying gas where the clown was. The cars lined up for a block. To keep people happy, Luis climbed and rolled all over people's cars. He cleaned people's sunglasses instead of their windows. And he made jokes with everyone. The radio and TV stations and the newspaper all did stories about the funny clown in the street. Luis was a star.

The only problem was money. At

$40 a week, it was going to take a long time to save up $600. So at the end of two weeks, Luis asked for a raise.

"Fifty dollars a week? Are you kidding?" Mr. Grogan asked.

"But I got you hundreds of new customers," Luis said.

"Yeah, I know. And now that I've got so many, who needs you? You're fired. Here's your pay and you can keep the clown costume."

Luis couldn't speak. He just put his clown costume and his makeup in a bag and he left.

"Where's the clown?" That's what everybody said to Mr. Grogan when they drove into the gas station the next week.

"Had to get rid of him," Mr. Grogan said. "He got to be a real pain in the neck."

At first, Mr. Grogan didn't notice, but one by one, all of his customers disappeared. Then one day he was driving down State Street and traffic was terribly slow.

"What's holding things up?" he grumbled to himself. He blasted his horn. "Hey! Let's get this show on the road!" But no one would move. "I'll take care of this," Mr. Grogan said, getting out of his car.

He stomped to the head of the long line of cars until he got to the corner. And there in front of Sam's Service Station was Luis. He was in the middle of the street, joking and wearing the clown costume. He was laughing and squirting people with his squirt gun and rolling on cars. He was telling everyone to "drive right on in to Sam's."

And business was booming.

READING CHECK

WORD MEANING FROM CONTEXT

1. Luis spent "three *solid* weeks" looking for a job. The word *solid* means _____ .
   a. having good sense
   b. time spent without a break
   c. hard

MAIN IDEA

2. This story is about someone who _____

   _____ .

DETAILS

3. To look like a clown, Luis had to _____

   _____ .

SEQUENCE

4. Luis started yelling at passing cars _____ .
   a. before he went to work for Mr. Grogan
   b. after the driver asked him what he was supposed to look like
   c. as soon as he put on his clown outfit

FINDING PROOF

5. The things Luis said and did made people go to Grogan's gas station.

Proof of this is _____ .

CAUSE AND EFFECT

6. People stopped going to Grogan's and started going to Sam's Service

Station because _____ .

WHAT DO YOU THINK?

Mr. Grogan gave Luis the idea of dressing like a clown and gave him the costume. But he wouldn't give him a raise. Was Luis right to play clown for another gas station? Should he have done something else to draw business to Sam's? If you were Mr. Grogan, what would you do to get your business back?

WHO SAID IT?

Sometimes in a story, two or three people have a **conversation**, or speak together. But you are not told who is speaking. You must read very carefully to figure this out.

Read the conversation that Ann, Lynn, Matt, and Tony have about going to the movies. The first paragraph below tells you about each person. These facts are your **clues.** Fill in the blanks with the names of the people who are speaking and to whom they are speaking. The first name has been filled in for you.

Lois thinks about love a lot. She reads love stories, and always hopes for a happy ending. Lynn gets all A's in science, and hopes to go to the moon someday. Tony is on the baseball team, and likes all other sports. He also likes to joke. Matt plays the piano and has a big record collection.

"Let's go to see *Days in Space*. I hear you can get some tips on how to build a spaceship yourself," said _____Lynn_____.

"Oh, no, there are no girls in it. Nobody falls in love or anything," said _____ .

"I'd like to see it. I hear they have a football game inside the space-ship," said _____ .

"Not me — everyone says the sound track is terrible. They just have squeaks and rattles instead of real music," said _____ .

"I'll tell you what," said _____ . "If you wait until I get through with the game, I'll go with you and hold your hand. That way there will be love in the picture. How about it, _____?"

"That sounds lovely, _____," said _____ softly.

"And I'll wire up a sound track that you can listen to with earplugs if you'll go with me, _____," said _____ .

"If you let me choose the music, I will," said _____ .

WHY DID THEY SAY IT?

You can tell a lot about a person from the things he or she says. What characters say in stories tell you what they think or feel. But sometimes you have to read carefully to understand what they *really* mean.

Here are some lines from "$40 a Week," and some questions about them. Choose the answer that best completes each statement.

1. **"You can start tomorrow if you want. It'll be a lot of fun," Mr. Grogan said without a smile."** Grogan meant _____ .
   a. "It's a great job."
   b. "The job is not right for you."
   c. "It's a rotten job, but you're lucky to get it."

2. **"I look like a fool," Luis said.** He was afraid that he would be _____ .
   a. stopped by police
   b. hurt
   c. laughed at and embarrassed

3. **"You're a little early for Halloween, aren't you?" the driver said with a snort.** He was trying to _____ .
   a. tell Luis the date
   b. insult Luis and make him mad
   c. be friendly

4. **"You're pretty funny for a clown," the driver said to Luis.** He

   was _____ .
   a. telling Luis he was good-looking
   b. praising Luis' sense of humor
   c. picking a fight

5. **"Drive that car in before you have to push it in!"**

   "You've got enough dirt on that car to plant a garden!"

   These are both insults meant to _____ .
   a. make people cry
   b. get a laugh
   c. show love

6. **"Grogan's gives you better gas than the high school cafeteria."**

   This is _____ .
   a. a tip not to buy gas at the school
   b. true and silly, so it makes people laugh
   c. a lie told to sell more gas

7. **"Fifty dollars a week? Are you kidding?" Mr. Grogan asked.**

   He meant _____ .
   a. "Luis, you said something funny."
   b. "You'll never get fifty dollars a week out of me."
   c. "I've never even earned fifty dollars a week."

8. **"He got to be a real pain in the neck," Mr. Grogan said.**

   Grogan was _____ .
   a. telling the truth
   b. in pain from a sore neck
   c. lying to save face

FUNNY COMEBACKS

"You're pretty funny for a clown," the driver said to Luis.
"You're laughing now, but wait till you see our prices," Luis said.

Luis made some pretty smart remarks in the story. Everybody laughed, and he was on his way to success.

Following are some other funny answers. Then there is a list of the questions, or statements, that they answer. Match them up. Write the letter of the question or statement next to each funny comeback.

Answers

_____ 1. Of course I do, but tell me more about Chuck.

_____ 2. I couldn't get her to date me, either.

_____ 3. Did you ever try to strike a match on a marshmallow?

_____ 4. All of them.

_____ 5. Must you always wait until the very last minute?

_____ 6. He came up to my chin one time too many.

_____ 7. It can't be midnight, because I was supposed to be home then, and I'm not.

_____ 8. Neither can I, but it doesn't keep me from talking.

Questions/Statements

a. In the ABC's, what letter comes after C?

b. What do you mean, answer the phone? It's not ringing.

c. Nothing you can think of is impossible.

d. I know I'm not good-looking like Chuck, and I don't have a car like his, but you love me, don't you?

e. You call yourself a fighter! You got knocked out by a man who only comes up to your chin!

f. I can never think of a thing to say.

g. What time is it?

h. That Sally is stuck-up, and dumb, and ugly.

END-OF-BOOK ACTIVITY

You've just finished the book. Now suppose you are on a train. As you go down the aisle, you hear bits of conversation between people sitting together. Here are the names of the people:

Bess (A Place to Call Home)
Grandfather (A Place to Call Home)
Jim (The Joyride)
Junior (The Lot)
Marie (Petty Thief)
Robbie (Today Is the First Day of...)
Harvey (Petty Thief)
The Genie (Today Is the First Day of...)
Mr. Grogan ($40 a Week)
Luis ($40 a Week)

Here are the bits of conversation you hear. Decide which person is speaking. Then decide to whom that person would be talking. Under each conversation, write the name of the speaker. Then write the name of the person spoken to.

"I'd like to meet your grandfather some day, but for me there's no tomorrow."

Speaker: _____

Speaking to: _____

"Hey, kid, that's a great suit you've got on — and that red nose is wild. This Lincoln Continental needs gas — which way is it to Sam's?"

Speaker: _____

Speaking to: _____

"Sure, I could get that clown kid to work for you again — your wish is my command."

Speaker: _____

Speaking to: _____

"Kid, take my advice. Get rid of that .22 pistol. I just read a diary by somebody who's going to get into trouble. I don't want to hear about any more."

Speaker: _____

Speaking to: _____

"What's the world coming to? My granddaughter wants to get rid of me. And now I see a beautiful girl like you stealing from people!"

Speaker: _____

Speaking to: _____

"I know how you must feel about cars — I can understand why you took one, once. With me, it's motorcycles — I had a big poster of one in my room — when I still had a room."

Speaker: _____

Speaking to: _____

VOCABULARY REVIEW

ambition	determined	official	spree
apologize	dreadful	perpetual	stunt
bolt	enlisted	petty	tightrope
cancelled	explode	promotion	weird
chef	holler	reflection	vacant
confused	impulse	risky	you're
decoy	license	sergeant	

Here are some words you learned as you read the stories in the book. On the next page are definitions for some of the words. Think of the word that best fits each definition. Then choose as your answer the *first letter* of that word.

Example: A synonym for the word *strange* is __W__ .

F   D   W   N   P

The sample sentence should bring to mind the word *weird*. Therefore, the letter W would be the correct answer.

Complete the following by writing the first letter of the word that fits the definition. When you are done, you will have part of the answer to the following riddle:

What is the tallest building in the world?

1. Something that is often "walked" in a circus is a _____.

    R S B T M

2. Another word for *scream* or *shout* is _____.

    C W E T H

3. *To burst out suddenly* is to _____.

    P E N U I

4. In order to drive, you must have a _____.

    L O V M K

5. Something done on the spur of the moment is done on _____.

    F L I A S

6. *To flee suddenly* is to _____.

    B J L E T

7. The opposite of *safe* is _____.

    Y S D R J

8. *Having goals for the future* is known as _____.

    D P A V T

9. A mirror image is a _____.

    R Y C F M

10. A word that means *you are* is _____.

    A I K D Y

You have the first part of the riddle answer. But you still may be wondering *why*. To end the suspense, complete the exercise on the last page.

Look at the list of words on _____ in each sentence below. The l_____ answer.

1. Because I enjoy _____

2. I will forgive you i_____

3. The crowd cheered at he_____

4. When I have money, I go on _____

5. The _ _ _ ☐ _ took their _____

6. My boss says that I can expect a _ _ _____ next year.

7. I have _ _ _ ☐ _ _ _ _ news. You _____

8. The picnic was _ _ ☐ _ _ _ _ _ _ due _____

9. Sometimes _ _ _ _ ☐ crimes lead to major crimes _____

10. The ☐ _ _ _ _ _ _ _ and the corporal met in the mess hall.

11. The stadium was _ _ _ _ _ ☐ the day after the last football game.

12. I received an ☐ _ _ _ _ _ _ _ letter from a senator.

13. He was _ _ _ _ ☐ _ _ _ _ to win, and he did!

14. My friend _ _ _ ☐ _ _ _ _ in the Air Force.

15. You seem to have a _ _ _ _ ☐ _ _ _ _ smile on your face. You are always so cheerful.

16. When you speak quickly, I get _ _ _ _ _ ☐ _ _.